Get the most from this book

This book will help you revise Unit B003 of the OCR GCSE Food and Nutrition specification. You can use the contents list on the next page to plan your revision, topic by topic. Tick each box when you have:

1 revised and understood a topic

2 tested yourself.

You can also keep track of your revision by ticking off each topic heading through the book. You may find it helpful to add your own notes as you work through each topic.

The answers to all the questions can be found at the back of the book.

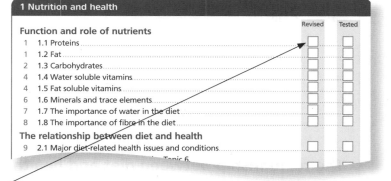

Tick to track your progress

examiner tips

Throughout the book there are exam tips that explain how you can boost your final grade.

Clear links back to the student book

Check your understanding

Use these questions at the end of each section to make sure that you have understood every topic.

Contents and revision planner

my revision notes

OCR
FOOD
NUTRITION

Anita Tull
Megan Pratt

HODDER
EDUCATION
AN HACHETTE UK COMPANY

Orders: please contact Bookpoint Ltd, 130 Milton Park, Abingdon, Oxon OX14 4SB. Telephone: (44) 01235 827720. Fax: (44) 01235 400454. Lines are open from 9:00 to 5:00, Monday to Saturday, with a 24-hour message-answering service. You can also order through our website www.hoddereducation. co.uk

If you have any comments to make about this, or any of our other titles, please send them to educationenquiries@hodder.co.uk

British Library Cataloguing in Publication Data
A catalogue record for this title is available from the British Library

ISBN: 978 1 444 18778 6
Published 2013.

Impression number 10 9 8 7 6 5 4 3 2 1
Year 2013, 2014, 2015, 2016, 2017

Hachette UK's policy is to use papers that are natural, renewable and recyclable products and made from wood grown in sustainable forests. The logging and manufacturing processes are expected to conform to the environmental regulations of the country of origin.

Typeset by Datapage (India) Pvt. Ltd.
Printed in Spain for Hodder Education, an Hachette UK Company, 338 Euston Road, London NW1 3BH.

4 Food preparation and cooking

5 Food safety and preservation

6 Consumer education

Acknowledgements

Every effort has been made to trace the copyright holders of material reproduced here. The authors and publishers would like to thank the following for permission to reproduce copyright illustrations.

Figure 1.2 © Ivan Mateev/iStockphoto.com; Figures 2.3 and 2.4 public sector information licensed under the Open Government Licence v1.0; Figure 4.1 © Eric Isselée – Fotolia; Figure 4.3 © John A. Rizzo/Photodisc/Getty Images; Figure 4.4 © Africa Studio – Fotolia; Figure 4.5 © Ingram Publishing Limited; Figure 5.1 reproduced with permission of the Soil Association; Figure 5.2 Hodder Education; Figure 7.1 © Imagestate Media (John Foxx); Figure 7.2 reproduced with permission of the Vegetarian Society; Figure 7.3 © kotoyamagami – Fotolia; Figure 7.4 © Brent Hofacker – Fotolia; Figure 7.5 reproduced with the permission of Coeliac UK; Figure 7.6 © Balint Radu – Fotolia; Figure 7.7 © Dr P. Marazzi/Science Photo Library; Figures 9.3 to 10. 3 Andrew Callaghan/Hodder Education; Figure 11.5 © David Toase/Photodisc/Getty Images; Figure 11.6 © Owen Price/iStockphoto.com; Figure 11.7 © M.studio – Fotolia; Figure 11.10 © Kesu – Fotolia; Figure 13.2 © helenlbuxton – Fotolia; Figure 13.3 reproduced with kind permission of Postharvest Technology Center, UC Davis – Plant Sciences; Figure 13.6 © Imagestate Media (John Foxx); Figure 13.7 © Lys - Fotolia.com; Figure 14.1 © Kurhan – Fotolia; Figure 15.1 © Photodisc/Getty Images; Figure 15.2 © Richard Gardner/Rex Features; Figure 16.2 © Siegfried Schnepf – Fotolia; Figure 17.2 (halal symbol) © design_things – Fotolia.

1.1–1.3 Nutrients: proteins, fat, carbohydrates

Key facts

- Food provides all the materials (**nutrients**) and **energy** that the body needs for growth, maintenance, repair and to work properly.
- Foods also contain (either natural or added): flavourings, colourings, enzymes, preservatives, texture.
- **Diet** is the food eaten every day.
- **Special diets** reduce or increase a nutrient or food, e.g. low salt diet, weight loss diet, high fibre diet.
- A **balanced diet** means eating right amounts of nutrients and a variety of foods for our individual needs.
- **Malnutrition** means 'bad' nutrition (too much or too little of one or more nutrients).

Proteins

- Protein molecules are made of **amino acids** – there are 10 **essential** amino acids that must come from food.
- **High biological value** (HBV) proteins contain all the essential amino acids.
- **Low biological value** (LBV) proteins are missing one or more of the essential amino acids.
- Mixing LBV proteins together supplies all the essential amino acids; this is called **protein complementing** (e.g. baked beans on toast).

Function (job) in the body	Found mainly in these foods	Result of deficiency (not enough)	
		Children	Adults
• growth • maintenance • repair and healing • energy	**HBV**: meat, fish, eggs, milk, cheese, soya beans, quinoa **LBV**: cereals, pulses, beans, some nuts, seeds, vegetarian alternatives, e.g. Quorn®	• poor growth • slow healing • catch infections easily • fluid under skin (oedema) • thin, weak • cannot digest food properly • diarrhoea • hair thinning	• lose muscle, fat • internal organs weaken • dry hair and skin • oedema

Fat

- Fat is **solid** at room temperature. Oil is a fat that is **liquid** at room temperature.
- Fat molecules are made of one part **glycerol** and three parts **fatty acids** – a **triglyceride**.

- **Saturated** fatty acids are full of hydrogen.
- **Unsaturated** fatty acids have double bonds and can take more hydrogen.
- **Monounsaturated** fatty acids have one double bond.
- **Polyunsaturated** fatty acids have two or more double bonds.
- **Hydrogenation** means adding hydrogen to make a liquid oil become a solid fat.
- Hydrogenation can make **trans fats**, which may be harmful to health.

Exam tip

You may be asked to state or describe ways someone can reduce their fat intake. A common exam mistake is to simply state 'eat less' or 'add less when cooking'; these are basic statements gaining limited marks. Try instead to think about:

- Different cooking methods – grilling rather than frying.
- Cutting off any visible fat.
- The type of foods chosen – lower fat options or leaner cuts of meat.

Function (job) in the body	Found mainly in these foods	Result of	
		Deficiency (not enough)	Eating too much
<ul><li>provides energy</li><li>stored in **adipose tissue cells**</li><li>insulates body from cold</li><li>protects organs (e.g. kidneys) and skeleton</li><li>provides vitamins A, D, E and K</li></ul>	**Visible fat**: butter, lard, suet, meat, margarine, nut and seed oils **Invisible fat**: oily fish, cheese, foods cooked in fat or oil, crisps and fried snack foods, nuts, egg yolk, cakes, pastries, biscuits, chocolate	<ul><li>deficiency of vitamins A, D, E and K</li><li>not enough essential fatty acids for growth of body tissues, especially in young children</li></ul>	<ul><li>if the energy provided by fat is not used up in physical activity it will be stored in adipose tissue</li><li>weight gain</li><li>fat can build up in the liver and cause health problems</li></ul>

Carbohydrates

Revised

- Carbohydrates are made by plants during **photosynthesis**.
- Carbohydrates provide the main source of energy for the body.
- One type, NSP (dietary fibre), helps the body get rid of solid waste.
- Complex carbohydrates or polysaccharides are made of long chains of **glucose** units joined together in different ways.

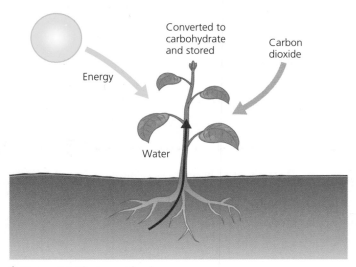

Energy

Converted to carbohydrate and stored

Carbon dioxide

Water

↑ Figure 1.1 Photosynthesis

The main food sources of carbohydrates:

Sugars	Complex carbohydrates (polysaccharides)
Monosaccharides: • **fructose**: fruits, plant juices, honey • **glucose**: vegetables, ripe fruits, sugar used in cooking • **galactose**: milk	**Starch**: root vegetables (carrots, parsnips), potatoes, yams, plantains, bananas, cereals (rice, wheat, millet, oats, maize, barley), cereal products (bread, bread products, pasta, breakfast cereals, pastries, biscuits, cakes), lentils, beans
Disaccharides: • **sucrose** (glucose and fructose): sugar (caster, granulated, brown); fruits and vegetables • **lactose**: milk and milk products	**NSP** (dietary fibre; includes cellulose, gums, which cannot be digested): wholegrain (wholemeal) cereal foods and cereal products, e.g. flour, bread, rice, oats, breakfast cereals, seeds, beans, lentils, fruits, vegetables
Maltose (glucose and glucose): cereals, e.g. barley, malted biscuits and milk drinks	**Pectin**: some fruits, e.g. plums, apricots, apples
Lactose (glucose and galactose): milk and milk products	**Dextrin**: toasted breads, pastries, cakes
	Glycogen: formed in the body, stored in the liver and muscles

A deficiency of carbohydrate (not enough) can cause:

● low blood glucose levels

● weight loss

● athletes to 'hit the wall'.

If you eat too much carbohydrate, it provides more energy than you will use up in physical activity. The rest will be stored in adipose tissue. This leads to weight gain.

Check your understanding

Tested

1	Name two high biological value (HBV) proteins.	*(2 marks)*
2	Give four reasons why the body needs protein.	*(4 marks)*
3	Give three reasons why the body needs fat.	*(3 marks)*
4	What is meant by the term 'invisible fat'?	*(1 mark)*
5	State two alternative names for sugar.	*(2 marks)*
6	Identify one good dietary source of NSP/fibre.	*(1 mark)*

1.4–1.5 Vitamins

The function and role of nutrients

Water soluble and fat soluble vitamins

Revised

- There are two groups of vitamins: water soluble (B group and C) and fat soluble (A, D, E, and K).
- Water soluble vitamins can be destroyed by heat and light or dissolve in cooking water.
- They are natural substances, needed in very small amounts.

Name	Function (job) in the body	Found mainly in these foods	Result of deficiency (not enough)
Water soluble vitamins			
Thiamin (vitamin B_1)	• releases energy from carbohydrates • body growth • helps nervous system	Yeast, yeast extract (Marmite®), cereals (especially wholegrain), cereal products, meat, eggs, milk, seeds, fish roe (eggs), nuts, beans	• wet or dry **beri-beri** • muscle wastage
Riboflavin (vitamin B_2)	• releases energy from carbohydrates, proteins and fats • body growth		• dry, cracked skin round mouth and nose • swollen tongue
Niacin (vitamin B_3)	• releases energy from carbohydrates • can lower blood fat levels	As above Can be made in the body from the amino acid tryptophan	**Pellagra** (three Ds: diarrhoea, dementia, dermatitis)
Pantothenic acid (vitamin B_5)	Releases energy from food	A wide range of foods	Rare
Pyridoxine (vitamin B_6)	Helps the body use protein, fat and carbohydrate	A wide range of foods (small amounts in each)	Headaches, weakness, aching, anaemia, skin problems
Folate (vitamin B_9) (folic acid is its man-made form)	• helps body use protein • helps make DNA in cells, especially in the bone marrow and digestive system • helps prevent spinal cord defects in unborn baby	Green and leafy vegetables, liver, potatoes, fruits (oranges, berries), asparagus, okra, beans, seeds, wholegrain cereals, nuts. Added to some breakfast cereals (fortification)	• nutrients not absorbed properly in digestive system (loss of appetite, nausea, diarrhoea, mouth soreness) • faulty bone marrow cells, resulting in large red blood cells that cannot deliver oxygen round body – this is **megaloblastic anaemia**
Cobalamin (vitamin B_{12})	• makes a protective coating around nerve cells • important for the correct production of new cells	Can be stored in the liver, found in animal foods (dairy foods, meat, fish, poultry) NOT found in plant foods – could be a problem for vegans	• nerves don't work properly, which leads to memory loss, confusion, paralysis • **pernicious anaemia**
Ascorbic acid (vitamin C)	• helps the body absorb iron from food • needed for the production of collagen, which makes connective tissue (which binds body cells together) • antioxidant – protects body from harmful chemicals • keeps skin and digestive system healthy	**Rich sources:** blackcurrants, citrus fruits (oranges, lemons, grapefruit, etc.), kiwi fruit, peppers **Important sources:** Brussels sprouts, broccoli, beansprouts, potatoes, peas, cabbage, leafy vegetables (not lettuce)	• anaemia (because iron not absorbed) • severe deficiency leads to **scurvy** (loose teeth, bleeding gums, red spots under skin [blood leakage from blood vessels], tiredness, weakness, weight loss, poor wound healing)

(Continued)

(Continued)

Name	Function (job) in the body	Found mainly in these foods	Result of deficiency (not enough)
Fat soluble vitamins			
Retinol (vitamin A, in animal foods)	<ul><li>body growth</li><li>healthy skin</li><li>keeps the mucous membranes in throat, the digestive system and the lungs moist and healthy</li><li>makes visual purple in the retina (night vision)</li><li>antioxidant – protects body from harmful chemicals</li></ul>	Dairy foods (milk, cheese, butter), egg yolk, oily fish (e.g. tuna, herring, mackerel, sardines), fish liver oils, liver, kidney	<ul><li>poor growth</li><li>frequent infections</li><li>night blindness, leading to…</li><li>irreversible blindness (**keratomalacia**)</li></ul>It is also a problem to eat too much vitamin A:<ul><li>poisonous to the body</li><li>pregnant women need to be careful</li><li>supplements only by medical advice</li></ul>
Beta carotene (vitamin A, in plant foods)		Margarine (added by law, by process called **fortification**), carrots, spinach, apricots, watercress, parsley, dark green leafy vegetables, tomatoes, palm fruit	
Cholecalciferol (vitamin D)	<ul><li>helps the body absorb calcium to make strong bones and teeth</li><li>important for making sure the bones reach **peak bone mass** (at their strongest)</li></ul>	<ul><li>fish liver oils, liver, oily fish, milk, butter, cheese, eggs, margarine (added by law)</li><li>made in the body by the reaction of sunlight (UV light) on the skin and stored in the liver</li></ul>	<ul><li>weak bones leading to **rickets** in children (**osteomalacia** in adults)</li><li>poor growth</li></ul>
Tocopherol (vitamin E)	<ul><li>antioxidant – protects body from harmful chemicals</li><li>keeps cell membranes healthy</li><li>helps protect against heart disease and cancer</li></ul>	Vegetable oils, lettuce, grasses, peanuts, seeds, wheatgerm oil	Rare
Vitamin K	Helps the blood to clot when the body is injured	<ul><li>leafy vegetables, cheese, liver, asparagus, coffee, bacon, green tea</li><li>made by bacteria in the intestines</li></ul>	<ul><li>rare in adults</li><li>may occur in newborn babies</li><li>all babies are given a dose when born</li></ul>

> **Exam tip**
>
> A common exam mistake is to identify the B group vitamins as 'vitamin B'. There is no such thing! Stating 'B group vitamins' or a specific B group vitamin, e.g. B_1 (thiamin), is correct.

Check your understanding   Tested

1 State three good sources of vitamin B_1 (thiamin).   *(3 marks)*

2 Describe the main functions of vitamin C.   *(4 marks)*

3 Identify the condition caused by a deficiency of vitamin A.   *(1 mark)*

4 Name two fat soluble vitamins.   *(2 marks)*

1.6–1.8 Minerals, water and fibre

The function and role of nutrients

Minerals and trace elements

Revised

- Adults need between 1mg and 100mg of **minerals** per day (calcium, iron, magnesium, phosphorus, potassium, sodium, chromium, copper, manganese, selenium, sulphur, zinc).
- Adults need less than 1mg of **trace elements** per day (fluoride, iodine, cobalt, molybdenum, silicon).

> **Exam tip**
>
> Be prepared to adapt a meal or diet to increase the intake of a given mineral, such as calcium or iron.

Name	Function (job) in the body	Found mainly in these foods	Result of deficiency (not enough)
Calcium	<ul><li>growth</li><li>makes strong teeth and bones</li><li>physical, load-bearing exercise stimulates the bones to take up minerals including calcium</li><li>especially important in childhood and adolescence</li><li>helps the blood to clot</li><li>keeps muscles and nerves working properly</li></ul>	<ul><li>vitamin D is needed to help the body absorb calcium from food</li><li>milk and dairy products (yogurt, cheese)</li><li>wholegrain cereals, seeds, nuts, lentils, green leafy vegetables</li><li>added to some foods to **enrich** them, e.g. soya milk, fruit juice, yogurt</li><li>**added to bread by law**</li></ul>	<ul><li>bones do not reach **peak bone mass**</li><li>bones gradually become weaker as people get older and are more likely to break</li><li>bones of pregnant women will weaken because calcium goes to baby</li><li>blood will not clot</li><li>nerves and muscles will not work properly – leads to **tetany**</li></ul>
Iron	<ul><li>helps produce **haemoglobin** in red blood cells, which carry oxygen around the body so energy can be produced in body cells</li><li>especially important for adolescent girls and women (**menstruation**)</li><li>pregnant women need extra to supply the baby</li><li>babies have a supply for the first three months of life</li></ul>	<ul><li>good sources: red meat, liver, kidney, corned beef, cocoa, plain chocolate, curry spices, dried fruit (especially apricots), lentils, treacle</li><li>some in egg yolk</li><li>green leafy vegetables – contain some iron but not all of it may be available to the body</li><li>often added to breakfast cereals (**fortified with iron**)</li><li>**added to bread by law**</li><li>vitamin C is needed to help the body absorb iron from food</li></ul>	Iron deficiency anaemia:<ul><li>tiredness</li><li>weakness</li><li>lack of energy</li><li>pale complexion</li><li>pale inner eyelids</li><li>weak or spilt fingernails</li></ul>
Sodium	<ul><li>controls amount of water in the body</li><li>helps the body use energy</li><li>helps control the nerves and muscles</li></ul>	<ul><li>salt (sodium chloride)</li><li>added to many foods – crisps, salted nuts, ready meals, takeaway foods, instant foods (e.g. soups), stock cubes, cheese, yeast extract (Marmite®), canned fish, smoked foods such as bacon</li><li>baking powder (sodium bicarbonate) in cakes, biscuits</li><li>monosodium glutamate, which increases the flavour of takeaway foods and ready meals</li><li>some bottled mineral waters have high sodium levels</li></ul>	<ul><li>muscle cramps (happens in hot conditions through sodium loss in sweat, or through sickness or diarrhoea)</li></ul>It is also a problem to eat too much sodium:<ul><li>most people eat too much salt</li><li>high blood pressure, which puts strain on the heart</li><li>kidney damage, especially in babies and young children</li></ul>
Fluoride	Strengthens enamel of teeth	<ul><li>sea water fish, tea, naturally found in some water supplies</li><li>added to some toothpaste brands</li></ul>	Teeth may develop more holes (cavities)
Iodine	Makes thyroid hormones, which control metabolic rate (rate of chemical reactions in body)	<ul><li>sea foods</li><li>milk, dairy foods, some plants (depending on the levels in the soil)</li></ul>	<ul><li>tiredness, lethargy</li><li>weight gain</li><li>**goitre** (thyroid gland swells up in neck)</li></ul>

The importance of water in the diet

● Water is essential for life (the body is approximately 60% water). Adults need to drink up to 2 litres per day – more in a hot climate or if very physically active.

● We get it by drinking and by eating naturally watery foods (fruits, vegetables, milk).

● Water is also added to some foods, e.g. soups, porridge, sauces.

↑ **Figure 1.2 Foods that contain water**

Function (job) in the body	Result of deficiency (not enough)	Result of excess
● found in all cells and tissues ● used for chemical reactions in body ● contained in all body fluids – blood, sweat, mucus, urine, joints, saliva, digestive juices ● removes waste products from the body – urine and faeces ● controls body temperature (sweating) ● used for digestion and the absorption of nutrients ● keeps blood concentration correct ● keeps skin moist	**Hypothalamus** in brain makes us feel thirsty Lack of water results in **dehydration**: ● headache ● dark, concentrated urine ● weakness, nausea ● overheating, confusion ● sunken eyes ● changes to blood pressure ● rapid heart beat ● loose, wrinkled skin ● a loss of 20% of body water will result in death Babies, young children, elderly people and kidney disease patients are vulnerable to dehydration	● water intoxication ● blood too diluted ● brain swells leading to headache, nausea, vomiting, muscle twitching, convulsions, death

The importance of fibre in the diet

- Non-starch polysaccharide (NSP) is known as fibre (fibre used to be called roughage).
- The ideal intake for adults is 30g a day (minimum 18g).

Exam tip

Fibre is not considered a nutrient as it passes through the body undigested.

Function (job) in the body	Where do we get it from?	Result of deficiency (not enough)
<ul><li>helps the body get rid of solid waste (**faeces**)</li><li>ensures intestines are healthy and work well</li><li>helps reduce the amount of **cholesterol** in the blood</li></ul>	**Cellulose**: stems, leaves, leaf stalks, seeds, beans, peas, lentils, fruits and vegetables (especially the skins), wholegrain (wholemeal) cereals and cereal products such as flour, breads, pasta, breakfast cereals, brown rice (which has seven times more fibre than white rice), oat or wheat bran, nuts **Pectin**: fruits such as plums, apples, blackcurrants	<ul><li>**constipation**, meaning the faeces are hard and difficult to expel from the body</li><li>this causes discomfort, bloating, tiredness due to waste products being held in body</li><li>**diverticular disease**, which causes pain and discomfort in the intestines. Small pouches develop in the intestinal lining, which can become infected with bacteria</li><li>increased risk of **cancer** in the **colon and rectum (colorectal cancer)**</li><li>drink plenty of water and exercise to keep intestines healthy and working properly</li></ul>

Check your understanding

1 State two good sources of iodine. *(2 marks)*

2 Describe the function of calcium in the diet. *(2 marks)*

3 How much water are we advised to drink per day? *(1 mark)*

4 Give three functions of water in the body. *(3 marks)*

5 State two functions of fibre. *(2 marks)*

2.1 The relationship between diet and health

Key terms Revised

- **Malnutrition** means the diet is unbalanced (too much or too little of one or more nutrients) and the person's health is affected.

- **Undernutrition** means not enough food is eaten to keep healthy.

- **Overnutrition** means eating too much food or too much of one or more nutrients, and a lack of exercise (in the UK and similar countries overnutrition is more common than undernutrition).

- A **risk factor** is doing or having something that makes you more likely to develop a diet-related health issue or condition.

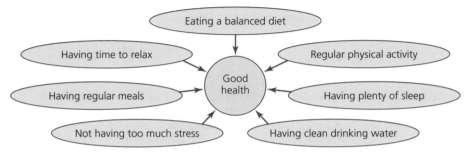

↑ **Figure 2.1 Factors for good health**

Overnutrition can lead to one of several diet-related health issues or conditions.

The reasons for increasing numbers of people developing diet-related health issues or conditions include:

- changing food habits; eating fewer fruit and vegetables and more processed foods; eating between meals ('snacking' and 'grazing'); eating too much

- less physical activity due to using cars or buses, sitting at a desk, watching TV, using computers, living in centrally heated homes, using labour-saving machines to do jobs.

Major diet-related health issues and conditions Revised

Health issue or condition	Risk factors	Key facts
Obesity (too much body fat)	• a lack of physical exercise • taking in more energy from food than the body uses • having other obese family members	• caused by taking in more energy from food than is used – energy is converted and stored as fat • many foods are energy-dense (they contain lots of fat and sugar) – they are easy to eat without realising what they contain • an increasing problem worldwide • obesity leads to: CHD, CVD, high blood pressure, stroke (blood clot in brain), arthritis, breathing problems, depression

(Continued)

(Continued)

Health issue or condition	Risk factors	Key facts
Coronary heart disease (CHD)	• high blood pressure • eating fatty, salty and sugary foods • being overweight or obese • smoking • drinking alcohol • stress • a lack of physical exercise	• the heart is a pump to move oxygen-rich blood around body • the heart muscle needs its own oxygen-rich blood supply from blood vessels called **coronary arteries** • blocked arteries caused by poor diet prevent the heart muscle receiving oxygen – this can lead to a heart attack • a high fat diet (especially saturated fats) can lead to blood vessel blockage
Cardiovascular disease (CVD)	• same as for CHD Also: • too much fat and cholesterol in blood • having fat around the waist	• blood vessels can become blocked anywhere in body – this restricts oxygen supply and damages vital organs, muscles, nerves, etc.
High blood pressure (hypertension)	• same as for CHD Also: • family history of high blood pressure	• a normal blood pressure reading for a healthy young adult is under 120 over 80 • high blood pressure is 140 over 90 or above • no symptoms • increases risk of developing CHD and CVD • salt increases blood pressure • people eat too much salt
Diabetes	• high blood pressure • eating fatty, salty and sugary foods • being overweight or obese • a lack of physical exercise • getting older	• **insulin** is needed to enable glucose in the blood to enter every cell of the body (insulin is like a key to unlock a door) • insulin is made in the **pancreas** • diabetes means the glucose stays in bloodstream and damages blood vessels • **symptoms**: thirst, frequent urination, tiredness, weight loss, blurred vision • **Type 1 diabetes** – usually diagnosed in children. The pancreas does not produce insulin, so injections have to be given every day and a balanced diet eaten • **Type 2 diabetes** – more common and increasing numbers of people are developing it due to bad diets and eating habits, being overweight or obese. The pancreas produces some insulin but the body cannot use it • there is **no cure** – if untreated diabetes can lead to serious illness and damage to the eyes (blindness), skin, blood vessels in hands and feet • should follow a **balanced diet** (eatwell plate)
Osteoporosis (porous bones)	• being overweight or obese • a lack of physical exercise • getting older • smoking • not enough calcium in diet • lots of fizzy drinks • family history of osteoporosis • drinking alcohol	• bones **mineralise** when young – most minerals are added during adolescence • **peak bone mass** is when bones are full of minerals (at 30–35 years) • the bones then gradually lose minerals (natural ageing process) • if peak bone mass is not achieved, the person is more likely to develop osteoporosis • when too many minerals have been lost, bones become brittle and break easily • a painful condition, causes spine to curve into a hump • **younger people** developing it due to poor diet, not enough physical activity, too many carbonated drinks
Cancer (growth disorder of abnormal body cells)	• diet • being overweight or obese • getting older • smoking • drinking alcohol • exposure to some chemicals	• a **tumour** is a cluster of cells growing in an uncontrolled way • can occur anywhere in the body • **carcinogens** are substances that can start the process of cancer • **reducing risk of developing cancer**: eat a healthy balanced diet with lots of fruit and vegetables and smaller amounts of red and processed meats; limit alcohol consumption; keep to a healthy weight; do not smoke

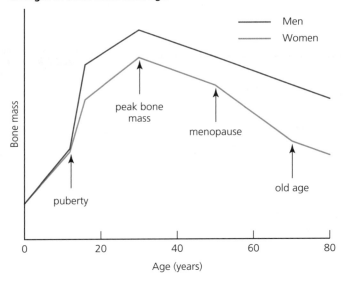

Changes in bone mass with age

Legend: Men, Women

(Graph labels: Bone mass (y-axis), Age (years) (x-axis); peak bone mass, menopause, old age, puberty)

↑ Figure 2.2 Changes in bone mass with age (source: Medical Research Council Human Nutrition Research)

Exam tip

You should be able to apply the information in this section. For example, a common question is: Describe four ways to reduce the risk of developing [named diet-related health issue or condition].

In order to answer this question, first think about each of the risk factors for the disease and then what steps you could take in day-to-day life to reduce these.

For example – one risk factor for diabetes is being overweight. So you could exercise more, which would help you lose weight by burning more calories, and this could also reduce your blood pressure and combat the risk factor of being inactive. You could also make links to healthy eating guidelines such as reducing salt intake, which would also help to reduce blood pressure.

Check your understanding   Tested

1 What does the term 'overnutrition' mean?   *(1 mark)*

2 Name three diet-related health issues or conditions.   *(3 marks)*

3 State four risk factors for the development of
   cardiovascular disease (CVD).   *(4 marks)*

2.2 Adapting meals and diets

The current dietary guidelines

Revised

- **Eight dietary guidelines** that apply to most people aged **over 5 years** in good health.

- **Do not apply** to very young children, babies, pregnant women or people with special health conditions.

- The **eatwell plate** is designed to help you follow guidelines:

The eatwell plate

Use the eatwell plate to help you get the balance right. It shows how much of what you eat should come from each food group.

FOOD
STANDARDS
AGENCY
food.gov.uk

Fruit and vegetables

Bread, rice, potatoes, pasta and other starchy foods

Meat, fish, eggs, beans and other non-dairy sources of protein

Foods and drinks high in fat and/or sugar

Milk and dairy foods

↑ **Figure 2.3 The eatwell plate**

Guideline	Why does it matter?	Other information
1. Base your meals on starchy foods	Most food on your plate should be a starchy plant food to give you energy	Includes: rice, pasta, potatoes (but not just chips), bread (wholemeal is best), oats, millet, cassava, yam, quinoa
2. Eat lots of fruit and vegetables	• to provide the body with a variety of vitamins, minerals, trace elements, fibre, antioxidants and other natural plant chemicals • a minimum of 5 portions a day recommended	1 portion is 80g, e.g.: • 1 apple, banana or orange • 2 plums or similar • 1 slice of melon, pineapple • 3 large tablespoons of vegetables or beans/lentils (pulses) or fruit salad • 1 large tablespoon dried fruit • 1 handful grapes/berries • 1 dessert bowl of salad • 1 glass (150ml) of fruit juice – **counts as maximum 1 portion a day**
3. Eat more fish	• provides a range of vitamins and minerals and protein • white fish is naturally low in fat • oily fish contains essential **omega 3 fatty acids** for a healthy heart • fresh fish has less salt than canned, dried or smoked fish	**Oily fish**: anchovies, salmon, trout, mackerel, herring, eel, sardines, kipper, fresh tuna **White fish**: cod, haddock, plaice, lemon sole, skate, hoki, hake, rock salmon (dogfish) **Shellfish**: prawns, shrimps, mussels, clams, crab, scallops

(Continued)

(Continued)

Guideline	Why does it matter?	Other information
4. Cut down on saturated fat (and eat less high fat foods)	• saturated fat is found in: butter, cheese, cream, coconut oil, palm oil, pastries, cakes, biscuits, chocolate, meat, meat products • fat in foods is often 'invisible'	**High fat foods**: have more than 20g fat in every 100g **Low fat foods**: have 3g or less fat per 100g **High saturated fat foods**: have more than 5g saturates per 100g **Low saturated fat foods**: have 1.5g or less saturates per 100g
5. Cut down on sugar	• most people eat too much sugar • sugars are often 'hidden' in drinks and other foods • chemical names are often used on labels, e.g. dextrose, glucose syrup, inverted sugar, hydrolysed starch – many people do not know these are sugars	• 50% daily energy should come from carbohydrate and only **11%** of that amount should come from sugars • excess sugar in the diet is converted to fat and stored in the body
6. Try to eat less salt	• many people eat too much salt • salt is used in a lot of processed foods	• adults should have no more than **6g** a day
7. Drink plenty of water	• most people do not drink enough water • approx. 2 litres a day should be drunk • drink more in hot countries, during physical activity and when ill	
8. Do not skip breakfast	• it is important to prepare the body for the day's activity • helps you feel alert, able to concentrate and less likely to eat snacks	• breakfast cereals often have large amounts of sugar and salt added • many cereals have vitamins and minerals added to make up for losses during processing
Additional guideline: Get active and try to be a healthy weight	• as important as food intake • helps maintain a healthy weight • makes heart, muscles, bones and immune system stronger • makes you feel good, confident, alert • helps reduce the risk of developing some diseases, e.g. heart disease, cancer	• everyday activities just as good as sport, e.g. walking, dancing, housework • if possible, walk or cycle instead of using the car or bus • get off the bus a couple of stops before your destination and walk • use the stairs rather than lifts or escalators • join a group for sport, walking or cycling for support

Buying your food

● Read and understand food labels.

● Use guidance systems on labels, e.g. traffic lights.

● Make and stick to a shopping list.

● Do not shop when you are hungry.

Preparing your food

● Try to adapt ingredients in a recipe to:

  • cut down fat, sugar and salt

  • increase fruits and vegetables

  • use alternative ingredients, e.g. wholemeal flour or pasta.

● Be aware of how much oil, sugar and salt you use.

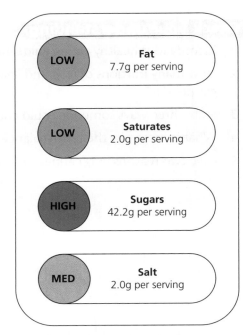

⬆ **Figure 2.4 Traffic light labelling**

Adaptation	How to do it
Reduce fat	• choose low fat or reduced fat versions of foods, e.g. canned fish, cheese, yogurt, low fat spreads, biscuits • choose lean meat • cut fat off meat • grill or oven bake instead of frying • when stir-frying, add a little water rather than more oil when the pan becomes dry • do not let food soak up oil when frying • use alternatives to mayonnaise, e.g. low fat crème fraîche • reduce the amount of butter or spread on bread
Reduce salt	• use alternative flavours, e.g. herbs, garlic, spices, lemon zest • buy reduced salt versions of foods such as crisps, baked beans • check labels for sodium content, e.g. in cakes (sodium bicarbonate), ready meals (monosodium glutamate) • eat naturally low salt fruits and vegetables, unsalted nuts
Reduce sugar	• reduce amount in recipes • use alternative sweet foods, e.g. carrots, ripe bananas, grapes • use sweeteners for flavour
Increase fibre and fruit and vegetables	• use wholegrain (whole meal) versions of foods • add oat bran, porridge oats or wheat bran to recipes • add dried fruits to recipes • eat fruits and vegetables with the skins left on • add peas, beans and lentils to recipes • add vegetables to meat dishes • add seeds to recipes • purée vegetables in soups, stews and sauces to 'disguise' them

Check your understanding — Tested

1 Identify four healthy eating guidelines.   (4 marks)

2 How many portions of fruit and vegetables is it recommended that we eat per day?   (1 mark)

3 State three ways someone could cut down their sugar intake.   (3 marks)

4 What is meant by the term 'balanced diet'?   (1 mark)

5 Give two reasons why eating a balanced diet may be difficult.   (2 marks)

2.3 Recommended daily amounts of nutrients

Dietary reference values (DRVs) — Revised

- DRVs are the amount of energy and nutrients different people need for growth and good health.
- People are grouped according to age, gender (male or female), pregnant or lactating (breastfeeding) females.
- DRVs only apply to healthy people – energy and nutrient needs change during illness or with a health condition.
- DRVs are used only for guidance – they are based on the needs of an average person.
- DRVs are helpful for people planning meals for groups of people, e.g. in schools, hospitals, residential homes, prisons.
- DRV figures for energy and nutrients are meant to be enough for 97% of a group of people.
- Food manufacturers show DRVs as **guideline daily amounts (GDAs)** on food labels.
- Energy values are given as kcals/kJ, and for adults as a percentage (%) of their daily energy intake.
- Macronutrient values are given as grams.
- Micronutrient values are given as:
  - milligrams – mg (1/1,000g)
  - micrograms – µg (1/1,000,000g).

Exam tip

You are not expected to learn each age group's DRVs, but you should be aware that these values differ for each group and the reasons for this. For example, a pregnant woman needs more protein and energy for the development and growth of the baby.

Fat and carbohydrates

- Adults should get 35% of their daily energy from fat, 11% from added sugars, and 39% from starches and natural sugars in their food.
- Adults are also recommended to eat 30g of fibre per day, or at least the very minimum 18g.

Protein and energy

Here are some extracts from the DRV tables for protein and energy. You can see the variation between people at different times of life. There are also differences between the genders.

Person	Protein DRV	Energy DRV (average)
Male, 7–10 years	28.3g	1,970 kcal
Female, 7–10 years	28.3g	1,740 kcal
Male, 19–50 years	55.5g	2,550 kcal
Female, 19–50 years	45g	1,940 kcal
During pregnancy	Add another 6g	Add 200 kcal
Male, over 75 years	53.3g	2,100 kcal
Female, over 75 years	46.5g	1,810 kcal

Micronutrients

There is a DRV for each vitamin and mineral. Here are some extracts from the DRV tables.

Person	Vitamin A	Vitamin C	Calcium
Male or female, 7–10 years	500µg	30mg	550mg
Male, over 19 years	700µg	40mg	700mg
Female, over 19 years	600µg	40mg	700mg
During pregnancy	Add 100µg	Add 10mg	No extra

Check your understanding   Tested

1   What does 'DRV' stand for?   *(1 mark)*

3 Energy and food

What is energy?

Revised

- Energy is needed by the body to work, move, keep warm, be active.
- **Basal metabolic rate (BMR)** is the amount of energy needed just to stay alive and keep everything in the body working.
- **Energy is used** by the body for: movement, producing heat and sound, chemical reactions, electrical energy (brain and nerves), storage of energy.
- Energy production in living cells is called **respiration**.
- **Oxygen** (from breathing) is needed to release the energy.
- When the energy is released, **water** and **carbon dioxide** (CO_2) are given off as waste products (breathed out).
- Factors that affect how much energy you need:
  - your age (more is needed when younger, less when older)
  - your activity levels (physical activities require a lot of energy)
  - your state of health (fighting an infection may increase energy needs as the body may use up fat stores; pregnant and lactating women need more energy)
  - your gender (usually – but not always – males need more energy than females).

Energy comes from the sun and is trapped by plants, which are then eaten by animals.

How is energy measured?

- Calories (cal) or joules (J)
- 1kJ = 1,000J
- 1 kcal = 1,000 cal
- 1 kcal = 4.2kJ

Sources of energy

- The main source is **carbohydrate**, which is broken down into **glucose** in the body. Glucose then travels to all cells in the bloodstream.
- Glucose is stored as **glycogen** in the liver and muscles to provide a **quick energy source**.
- **Fat** supplies energy, but it must be changed to glucose in the body first – this takes longer.
- Energy is stored as fat in **adipose tissue**.
- **Protein** can provide energy, but the body prefers to use protein for growth and repair.
- Different foods have different **energy values**.
- **Energy-dense foods** contain a lot of energy per gram. They are often high in fat and/or sugar.

↑ **Figure 3.1 Where energy comes from**

Source	Amount of energy
1g pure carbohydrate	provides 15.7kJ / 3.75 kcal
1g pure fat	provides 37.8kJ / 9.0 kcal
1g pure protein	provides 16.8kJ / 4.0 kcal
1g pure alcohol	provides 29.4kJ / 7.0 kcal

Energy requirements

- More physically active people need more energy.
- Energy requirements decrease as we get older.
- When young, energy is needed to make the body grow and be active.
- Physical activities that use a **lot of energy** include running, climbing, swimming, digging, lifting heavy weights, cycling, walking fast or uphill.
- Physical activities that use **very little energy (sedentary activities)** include sitting in a chair, watching TV, driving a car, using a computer.

> **Exam tip**
>
> The topic of energy and food is often linked to factors that influence energy requirements. Make sure you can describe why people's energy requirements are different. Think about meal adaption, for example adapting a meal/diet for someone trying to lose weight.

Energy balance

Energy intake over a period of time	Effect on body
Equal to energy used for all body activities	Weight stays the same
Less than energy used for all body activities	Loses weight
More than energy used for all body activities	Gains weight

Weight gain and weight loss do not happen quickly.

Someone trying to lose weight should aim to **increase their physical activity**, **eat less** energy-dense foods and lose **0.5–1kg** a week.

> **Check your understanding**   Tested
>
> 1 Describe three factors that influence an individual's energy requirement.   *(6 marks)*
>
> 2 State the units used for measurement of energy.   *(1 mark)*
>
> 3 What will happen if someone has a higher energy intake than expenditure?   *(1 mark)*
>
> 4 If someone has a higher energy intake than expenditure, what will the effect be on their health?   *(1 mark)*

4.1–4.2 Meat, poultry, fish and seafood

Meat and poultry
Revised

- Meat is the muscle fibres that come from animals and birds (poultry).
- It also includes internal organs such as the liver, kidneys (called **offal**).
- The nutritional value varies according to the age of the animal or bird and how it was reared (what it was fed on, how much it moved around, how quickly it grew).
- Cooking meat makes it easier to digest and absorb nutrients.

↑ Figure 4.1

Main nutrients	Buying advice	Storage
<ul><li>HBV protein</li><li>fat (mostly saturated), found under skin and between muscle fibres</li><li>vitamins A (especially liver), B group and D</li><li>iron, especially in red meat and liver</li><li>water (naturally occurring and some added)</li></ul>	Meat, poultry or offal should have:<ul><li>moist (not slimy or wet) texture</li><li>firm, slightly springy flesh</li><li>good colour</li><li>fresh smell</li></ul>It should not be past its use by date	<ul><li>perishable (goes 'off' quickly)</li><li>remove plastic packaging</li><li>store at 0°C–5°C</li><li>use within 1–2 days</li><li>to freeze: wrap meat well to prevent freezer burn</li><li>fast freeze to at least −18°C</li><li>defrost on a tray in the bottom of refrigerator for several hours</li><li>cool cooked meat dishes rapidly and refrigerate or freeze</li><li>reheat leftover meat dishes only once to at least 70°C</li></ul>

Fish and seafood
Revised

- Either caught from seas, lakes or rivers, or farmed in large cages.
- Eaten whole, cut into fillets or thick slices (steaks, sometimes called darnes).

Type	Examples	Description
Flat white fish	Plaice, sole, halibut	Firm white flesh Oil in the liver, but not the flesh
Round white fish	Cod, haddock, monkfish, hoki	
Oily fish	Anchovies, eel, herring, salmon, tuna	Quite dark flesh Oil in the flesh
Mollusc	Mussels, clams, oysters, squid	Soft-bodied sea animals Live inside shells (except squid and cuttlefish)
Crustaceans	Lobster, prawns, crab	Jointed sea animals Soft bodies covered by a hard outer skeleton

Main nutrients in fish

- HBV protein; this is easily digested.
- Fat (mostly unsaturated oils); found in the skin of oily fish and liver of white fish. An important source of omega 3 and omega 6 fatty acids.
- Vitamins A and D (especially oily fish) and B group.
- Calcium; in the bones of fish if eaten.
- Fluoride and iodine; especially in sea fish.
- Water; naturally occurring and some added.

Guidelines for buying good quality fish

Fish	Crustaceans	Molluscs
Firm, slightly springy flesh	Firm, springy flesh	
Fresh smell	Fresh, 'sweet' smell	Fresh smell
• moist (not slimy or wet) skin • good colour	Moist	
• clear, shiny eyes • not losing lots of scales • bright red gills	No missing joints or limbs	Tightly shut shells
Not past its use by date		

Storage of fish and shellfish

- Perishable (goes 'off 'quickly).
- Remove plastic packaging.
- Store at 0°C–5°C.
- Use within 1 day.
- To freeze (must be done on day of purchase): wrap fish well to prevent freezer burn.
- If previously frozen, do not refreeze (check with shop).
- Fast freeze to at least −18°C.
- Defrost on a tray in the bottom of refrigerator for several hours.
- Cool cooked fish dishes rapidly and refrigerate or freeze.
- Reheat leftover fish dishes only once to at least 70°C.

Check your understanding
Tested

1. State three nutrients found in meat. *(3 marks)*
2. Give one reason why a pregnant woman should not eat liver. *(1 mark)*
3. Describe how you would check if a chicken was thoroughly cooked. *(2 marks)*
4. Identify three nutrients found in fish. *(3 marks)*
5. Give two reasons people are recommended to eat more oily fish. *(2 marks)*

4.3–4.5 Eggs, milk and dairy products

Eggs

- Main types eaten are hen, duck, goose, quail.
- Battery eggs come from hens kept in cages.
- Free range eggs come from hens that have freedom to move about outside.
- Barn or perchery eggs come from hens kept in large barns with perches.
- Keep in refrigerator away from strong-smelling foods.
- If an egg shell is dirty, wash your hands after touching it.

Nutrients in eggs

- HBV protein in white and yolk; this is easily digested.
- Fat is found in the yolk.
- Vitamins A, D and E are found in the yolk, and B group (especially B_2 and B_{12}) in the white and yolk.
- Phosphorus, zinc and selenium found in the white, and iron in the yolk.
- Water; naturally occurring in the white and yolk.

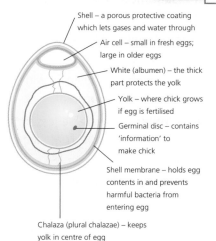

Shell – a porous protective coating which lets gases and water through

Air cell – small in fresh eggs; large in older eggs

White (albumen) – the thick part protects the yolk

Yolk – where chick grows if egg is fertilised

Germinal disc – contains 'information' to make chick

Shell membrane – holds egg contents in and prevents harmful bacteria from entering egg

Chalaza (plural chalazae) – keeps yolk in centre of egg

⬆ **Figure 4.2**

> **Exam tip**
>
> Questions about eggs often relate to how eggs are cooked and the functions of eggs.

Milk

- The main types used are cow's, goat's, sheep's.
- Produced by mammals.
- Designed to provide a baby mammal with all it needs, therefore milk is very nutritious.
- Milk is **homogenised** (the fat is broken up into tiny droplets).
- Milk is very **perishable** as it has the right conditions for bacteria to grow.
- It is **heat-treated** to destroy harmful bacteria.

Heat treatment and storage of milk

- **Pasteurisation**: milk is heated quickly in a heat exchanger to **72°C for 15 seconds**. It is then cooled quickly to **4°C**. **HTST** means high temperature, short time pasteurisation. Refrigerate this milk and use it within a few days.

- **Ultra Heat Treated (UHT)**: milk is quickly heated in a heat exchanger to **132°C for 1 second**. It is then cooled quickly and packed in special sealed packs. It can be stored at room temperature, **unopened**, for several months. Once opened, store this milk in the refrigerator as for fresh milk.

- **Dried milk**: milk is dried and stored in packs to be made up with water.

- **Canned milk**: milk is **evaporated** (the water is removed) by heat then canned. **Condensed** milk is evaporated, has sugar added, then is canned.

Types of milk

- **Whole milk** has no fat removed (it is approximately 3.9% fat). It is usually sold in **blue**-labelled bottles.

- **Semi-skimmed milk** is 1.5% fat. It is usually sold in **green**-labelled bottles.

- **Skimmed milk** is 0.1% fat (virtually fat-free). It is usually sold in **red**-labelled bottles.

- It is also possible to buy milk with approximately 1% fat (may be sold in **purple**-labelled bottles).

- **Other 'milks'** are available (e.g. for people with allergies, or vegans): soya, oat, rice, coconut. These are often enriched with vitamins and minerals.

Main nutrients in milk

- HBV protein; this is easily digested.

- Fat; a mixture of saturated and unsaturated depending on what the cow has eaten.

- Carbohydrate (lactose).

- Vitamins A and D (more in summer if the cows are outside), B group, very little vitamin C.

- Calcium, phosphorus, sodium, potassium. Very little iron.

- Water; milk is about 90% water.

> **Exam tip**
>
> In previous exams some candidates have stated 'blue top milk', which is considered too vague. Always use specific terms such as 'whole milk'.

Dairy products
Revised

Cheese

Type of cheese	Examples	Additional information
Soft cheese (fresh)	Cream cheese, cottage cheese, mozzarella	
Soft cheese (ripened)	Camembert, Brie, goat's cheese	
Blue-veined cheese	Blue Stilton, Danish blue	Edible mould is added, giving a distinct flavour and blue 'veins'
Semi-soft cheese	Stilton, Wensleydale, Lancashire, Edam	
Hard cheese	Cheddar, Gruyère, double Gloucester	
Very hard cheese	Parmesan	
Whey cheese	Ricotta	Made from whey with additional ingredients such as milk
Processed cheese	Cheese slices, cheese spreads	Made by mixing pieces of cheeses and colouring

Main nutrients in cheese (varying in quantity according to type of cheese):

- HBV protein; this is easily digested.

- Fat; a mixture of saturated and unsaturated depending on what cow has eaten (hard cheeses are 33% fat, full fat cream cheese 50%, cottage cheese 4%).

- Vitamins A and D (more in summer if the cows are outside), B group.

- Calcium, phosphorus, sodium.
- Water; hard cheeses are 33% water, soft cheeses up to 80%.

Buying and storing cheese:

- Perishable, especially soft cheeses.
- Make sure packaging is not damaged.
- Store at 0°C–5°C in sealed box to prevent drying.

Cream

- Cream is small droplets of butterfat suspended in a liquid.
- Cream is skimmed off milk at 35°C–54°C, then cooled to 4°C.

Type of cream	Fat content	Examples of use
Double	48%	Whipping Decorating cakes Adding to soups or sauces
Whipping	38%	Whipping Decorating cakes
Single	18%	Pouring Adding to soups or sauces
Soured	Up to 20%	Dips Jacket potato toppings
Crème fraîche	Up to 35%	Served with desserts Used in cheesecake
Clotted	55%	Served with scones (cream tea) or desserts
Ready 'whipped' (with added sugar, stabilisers and gas)	Depends on type	Sold in cans; heat treated to increase shelf life Decorating cakes and desserts

↑ Figure 4.3 Whipping cream

Main nutrients in cream:

- HBV protein (small amount only).
- Fat; mostly saturated.
- Vitamins A and D (more in summer if the cows are outside), small amounts of B group.
- Some calcium, and other minerals and trace elements.
- Water; some naturally occurring.

Storing cream:

- Very perishable, cover and store in refrigerator and use within a few days.
- Whipped cream (double and whipping) can be frozen.

Butter

- Made from cream.
- Made by 'churning' (stirring) cream to make butterfat droplets stick together and watery buttermilk to separate.

Main nutrients in butter:

- HBV protein (very small amount).
- Fat; mostly saturated.
- Vitamins A and D (more in summer if the cows are outside).

Type of butter	Description
Unsalted ('sweet')	Mild, slightly sweet
Salted	Salt is the only added ingredient (traditionally as a preservative, now for flavour)
Clarified	Used in butter sauces and for shallow frying Made by slowly melting butter, skimming off the milk solids to leave only the melted fat
Ghee	Clarified butter that originated in India Has a strong flavour Sold in cans
Spreadable	Vegetable oils are added so that the butter stays soft when refrigerated

● Some minerals and trace elements, including sodium from added salt.

● Water (very small amount).

Storing butter:

● Can be kept in a covered dish at room temperature (not too warm) for spreading.

● Store in a refrigerator for other uses.

Yogurt

● Yogurt is cultured milk (special bacteria have been added).

● Bacteria produce lactic acid to coagulate (set) the protein in the milk and to flavour the yogurt.

● Eaten as natural or flavoured yogurt.

Type of yogurt	Description	Flavour
Set	Semi-solid (it is set in the pot it is bought in)	Sold natural or flavoured
Stirred	Varies in thickness; can be poured	Sold natural or flavoured
Natural (plain)	Smooth, creamy texture	Fresh, tangy flavour
Greek (strained)	Made from cow's or sheep's milk High fat content	Mild flavour
Live	The bacteria in this yogurt are still living	

Main nutrients in yogurt:

● HBV protein; a good source.

● Fat; many types are low-fat but some have cream added.

● Carbohydrate; some lactose plus added sucrose and fructose in flavoured yogurt.

● Vitamins A and D (more in summer if the cows are outside), some B group vitamins.

● Good source of calcium.

● Water; a good source.

Buying and storing yogurt:

● Perishable.

● Check the use by date.

● Make sure lid has not 'blown' (means yeast contamination has caused fermentation of the sugar in flavoured yogurts).

● Store in refrigerator.

Check your understanding

Tested

1 Circle the nutrients egg is a good source of. *(5 marks)*

   Protein   Fluoride   Fibre   Fat   Vitamin A   Calcium   Iron

2 Identify two fat soluble vitamins found in cow's milk. *(2 marks)*

3 State two types of milk someone intolerant to lactose could consume instead of cow's milk. *(2 marks)*

4 Cream is a perishable food. What is meant by the term 'perishable food'? *(1 mark)*

5 Identify two checks you could make when buying yogurt to check that the product is of an acceptable quality. *(2 marks)*

4.6 Fruits and vegetables

Key facts

- An important part of the diet – a minimum of five portions a day is recommended.

- Uses: can be eaten on their own (many raw with or without skins and seeds); as side dishes or part of many recipes; in sauces, drinks, soups, stocks; as flavourings; as garnishes; to give texture and colour.

- Cooking can destroy vitamins (especially vitamin C). To conserve vitamins, the chosen cooking method should be for the shortest time, in a minimum amount of water until the fruit or vegetable is just tender. Serve immediately.

- Many can be frozen (not very watery ones, e.g. lettuce, cucumber), canned or dried.

Type of fruit	Examples
Soft berry fruits	Raspberries, strawberries
Currants	Blackcurrants
Hard fruits	Apples, pears
Stone fruits	Plums, apricots
Citrus fruits	Oranges, lemons
Exotic fruits	Banana, passionfruit, kiwi fruit

↑ **Figure 4.4 A selection of fruit**

Type of vegetables	Examples
Roots	Carrots, beetroot
Tubers (attached to roots)	Potatoes, sweet potatoes
Bulbs	Onions, leeks
Stems	Asparagus, celery
Leaves	Cabbage, lettuce
Flower heads	Cauliflower, broccoli
Fungi	Mushrooms
Legumes (really seeds but used as vegetables)	Peas, broad beans, lentils, bean sprouts
Vegetable fruits	Tomatoes, peppers

↑ **Figure 4.5**

Main nutrients in fruits and vegetables

● LBV protein; in peas, beans, lentils (HBV in soya beans).

● Fat; some in peas, beans and lentils; more in avocados, nuts, sweetcorn.

● Carbohydrate; made during photosynthesis in green plants, as sugars, starch, fibre (NSP).

● Vitamins C (a rich source), A (as beta carotene), some B group, some E.

● Minerals and trace elements; the quantity and range depends on where the plants grow and the quality of the soil.

● Water; a very important source.

● Fibre; a very good source.

● Also contain other important substances that benefit our health such as **antioxidants**.

Buying and storing fruits and vegetables

● Avoid bruised, mouldy, damaged, soft or wilted ones.

● Nutritional value, texture and flavour decrease after harvesting and picking, so use up soon after purchase.

● Store in a cool, dark place (potatoes go green if left in light and become poisonous to eat). Some, e.g. bananas and potatoes, go black if they are too cold).

● Always wash before using and eating.

> **Exam tip**
>
> Fruit and vegetable intake is an important area and is covered in many topics. Ensure that you can link it to other areas such as healthy eating, reducing the risk of some diseases and illnesses and encouraging people to increase their intake.

Check your understanding   Tested

1 Identify two fruits or vegetables that are a good source of beta carotene. *(2 marks)*

2 Identify three ways to encourage a toddler to eat more fruit and vegetables. *(3 marks)*

3 State three things you should consider when buying and storing fruits and vegetables. *(3 marks)*

4.7 Cereals and cereal products

Key facts

Cereals are:

- grains (seeds); mostly from cultivated grasses
- a **staple** food around the world
- a major source of **energy**.

Most seeds are **processed** by milling into flour.

- Some nutrients are lost during processing.
- White flour has 30% of the seed removed, it contains **70% of the grain**.
- Wholemeal (wholegrain) flour has none of the seed removed, it contains **100% of the grain**.
- Tough outer layers (husks) are removed from rice by 'polishing'; from barley by 'pearling'; from oats by 'hulling'.
- **Breads** are commonly made from cereal flours as a nutritious and filling part of a meal (loaves, rolls, sandwiches, wraps, tortillas, pittas, naans).
    - Unleavened bread is flat, not risen by yeast.
    - Leavened bread is risen by yeast. Needs strong plain flour with a high gluten content to make dough stretch and rise (that flour is also needed for choux and puff/flaky pastry).
- **Cakes, other pastries and biscuits** need soft plain flour (less gluten).

Nutrients in cereals

Whole seeds are very nutritious because they contain all the nutrients for plant growth:

- LBV protein.
- Fat (a small amount).
- Carbohydrate; starch and NSP (wholegrain).
- B group vitamins and vitamin E.
- Iron.
- A variety of trace elements.

> **Exam tip**
>
> 'Cereal' does not simply refer to breakfast cereals. Think of all the grains available in different cultures.

> **Exam tip**
>
> Bran, endosperm and germ are the three main parts of a cereal grain. Make sure you can label them on a diagram.

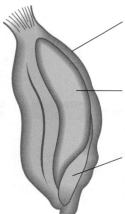

Bran – most fibre (NSP) found here; many vitamins, minerals and trace elements; some protein and fat

Endosperm – carbohydrate (starch); most protein found here; some vitamins

Germ – contains genetic information for a new plant to grow from seed; most of the fat and some protein, vitamins and trace elements found here

↑ **Figure 4.6**

Types of cereal and their uses

Cereal	Uses	Important nutrients	Contains gluten?
Barley	• animal feed • beer and whisky • bread • soups and stews • breakfast cereals • malt (sweetener in foods, maltose)		Yes
Buckwheat	• flour • pasta • eaten like rice	Good source of calcium	No
Corn (maize)	• animal feed • corn oil • high fructose corn syrup (sweetener for fizzy drinks) • cornflour (thickener for sauces) • cornmeal (polenta), for breads, cakes, biscuits, tortillas, muffins, fried snack foods • sweetcorn, corn on the cob (vegetable) • popcorn		No
Millet	• breakfast cereals • porridge	Good source of iron	No
Oats	• oatmeal • porridge oats or jumbo oats used for porridge • oats or oat bran added to breads, cakes, crumbles, biscuits, oatcakes, flapjacks, oat crackers	Good source of calcium	A little
Quinoa	Used as an alternative to rice	Rich in protein	No
Rice	Many varieties; used in many sweet and savoury dishes	Very important for energy and B vitamins	No
Rye	• bread • breakfast cereals		Yes
Spelt	• bread • pasta	More protein than wheat	Yes, but different structure so can be eaten by some people with allergy to ordinary wheat
Wheat	Very important cereal • all baked products (breads, pastries, cakes, biscuits, puddings) • breakfast cereals • bulgur wheat eaten like rice • couscous from durum wheat (used for pasta) • wheat bran and wheat germ added to recipes • wheat products, e.g. semolina, added to cakes, biscuits, puddings		Yes

Check your understanding
Tested

1 Identify four nutrients found in cereals.   (4 marks)

2 Name three types of cereal grain.   (3 marks)

3 State why a coeliac cannot eat bread made from wheat flour.   (1 mark)

4.8 Sugars and sweeteners

Key facts

- Sugar is used as a sweetener and preservative.
- Cane sugar (sucrose) is produced from a very tall grass (tropical climates).
- Beet sugar (sucrose) is produced from a plant root (temperate climates).
- Used in recipes to give colour (caramelisation) and texture (aeration).
- Can damage teeth and lead to obesity if eaten in excess.
- Most recipes will work if sugar content is reduced.
- Sweet alternative foods can be used in recipes, e.g. dried fruits, carrots, ripe fresh fruits.
- Artificial food sweeteners add flavour but no sugar, e.g. saccharin, aspartame (dangerous for people with PKU/phenylketonuria), acesulfame K, sucralose.

> **Exam tip**
>
> Questions often focus on ways to reduce sugar intake or how to identify sugar on food labels.

Main nutrients in sugars

- Carbohydrate and natural refined sugars (e.g. sucrose) are 100% carbohydrate.
- Minerals and trace elements; some iron and calcium found in brown sugars (in molasses); honeys contain varying amounts.
- Some B group vitamins found in honeys.

Type of sugar	Description
Muscovado (molasses) sugar	Dark brown, strong flavour, moist Small, fine crystals
Demerara (raw) sugar	Light brown, slightly moist, contains some molasses Medium crystals making it 'crunchy'
Light, soft brown sugar	Light brown, 'syrupy' flavour Fine crystals
White granulated sugar	Refined (no molasses), used for all purposes Medium crystals
White caster (superfine) sugar	Refined (no molasses) Very small crystals
Icing (confectioner's) sugar	White (no molasses) Ground into a fine powder

Type of syrup	Description
Maple syrup	Made from the sap of the maple tree Distinctive flavour, sweeter than sugar
Golden syrup	Made from cane sugar Light, golden colour with distinctive flavour
Black treacle	Made from refined molasses Thick, black, very sticky, with very strong, slightly bitter flavour
Molasses	Varies in colour and thickness Usually contains minerals and trace elements

Check your understanding

Tested

1   State three functions of sugar.   (3 marks)

2   Identify two ways to reduce the sugar content of a Victoria sponge recipe.   (2 marks)

5.1–5.3 Convenience, genetically modified and organic foods

Convenience foods
Revised

● Definition: food products made by manufacturers and designed to save consumers time and effort when making meals.

Advantages	Disadvantages
Designed to make meal planning and preparation easier Save time and effort No specific cooking skills needed Have a long shelf-life Sold in portion-controlled sizes Useful for people who: ● are physically disabled ● cook only for themselves ● have limited kitchen facilities ● work in catering companies	Tend to use lots of packaging, therefore cause environmental and sustainability problems Often have a high fat, sugar and salt content which may be 'hidden' in foods May contain additives Reduce the need for cooking skills resulting in fewer people knowing how to cook

Types of convenience foods

● **Meals**: complete (ready-to-eat); cook-chill; frozen; bottled; canned; dried; fast foods; take-aways.

● **Parts of meals**: sauces; soups; salads; vegetables; desserts; meat and fish products; cakes; pastas.

● **Ingredients**: stocks; packet mixes (batters, desserts, biscuits, burgers, breads); pastry; pizza bases; sandwich fillings, whipped cream, sauces.

> **Exam tip**
>
> Remember to use the knowledge gaining during the controlled assessment tasks and your own experience.
>
> Think of a product such as scones made from scratch, from a packet mix and ready-made. Think about the advantages and disadvantages of each. Are there any limitations to each method? For example, could someone with limited cooking skills or space make scones from scratch? Think about cost, time, facilities available, skills needed, taste, nutritional value and shelf life.

Genetically modified (GM) foods
Revised

● Genes control the characteristics of plants and animals.

● Genes are made of DNA containing four amino acids in different sequences to form a code of instructions for each characteristic.

● Genetic modification copies a gene for a specific characteristic from a plant or animal and inserts it into another plant or animal, where it is then reproduced.

● GM foods include soya beans, sweetcorn, sugar, rapeseed, tomatoes, rice.

Advantages of GM foods	Disadvantages of GM foods
• resistance to weed-killing chemicals • increased storage or shelf life • better resistance to insects, fungi and bacteria which would harm a crop • faster growing rates • less fat • better resistance to disease	• effects on the ecology of the area where they grow • development of resistant micro-organisms • development of allergies if DNA from certain plants and animals are put into others • infertile GM seeds means farmers have to buy new seeds from GM companies every year

Organic foods

● Organic plant foods have been grown using farming methods where plants are grown in well-balanced, healthy, living soil without the regular use of pesticides and fertilisers.

● Organic animal foods are reared in natural surroundings without the routine use of medicines (unlike intensive farming where animals are housed in large numbers inside production units).

● 'Organic' has a legal definition and foods have a symbol to certify they are organic.

● Organic foods are sold in most supermarkets, farmers' markets, farm shops, box schemes (delivered to your home or a collection point), and mail order.

↑ Figure 5.1

Exam tip

Currently, the question of whether organic foods have a better nutritional value than their non-organic counterparts is highly contested by scientists; some studies suggest it does, while others suggest it does not. Therefore, stating that 'organic food has more minerals/vitamins/nutrients' is incorrect and will not be credited. Stating that 'some studies have suggested they have a better nutritional quality ...' would be credited.

Advantages of organic foods	Disadvantages of organic foods
• considered to taste better because they are grown naturally in good soils • considered to be better for health because pesticides are not used • better for the environment and ecosystems	• often more expensive than intensively grown foods • many have to be imported, which has implications for transport pollution

↑ Figure 5.2

Check your understanding

1 Describe two advantages and two disadvantages of convenience foods. *(8 marks)*

2 State two advantages of genetically modified food for consumers and/or manufacturers. *(2 marks)*

3 State two reasons for the increased popularity of organic food. *(2 marks)*

4 What is meant by the term 'organic food'? *(1 mark)*

5.4 Functional foods

Key facts

- Definition: foods eaten as part of a normal diet that contain natural substances known to lower the risk of developing certain diseases and to maintain good health.
- Plant foods contain many natural substances (**phytochemicals**) that give them their colour, flavour, texture, smell, acidity and nutritional value.
- Some phytochemicals are thought to be active in the human body and very beneficial to health, e.g. as antioxidants.

Exam tip

Functional foods are a limited part of the specification. Your revision should concentrate on understanding what a functional food is and their role.

Many plant foods contain phytochemicals. These are just a few examples:

- onions, garlic and shallots
- broccoli, Brussels sprouts and cauliflower
- blueberries and blackcurrants
- wholegrain cereals.

Functional food	Suggested health benefits
Whole oats and oat products; foods made from soya beans; special margarines, e.g. Benecol®	Lower blood cholesterol and reduce the risk of developing heart disease
Oily fish containing omega 3 fatty acids	Reduces the risk of developing heart disease
Cranberry juice	Reduces the risk of developing urinary tract infections
Garlic	Lowers blood cholesterol levels
Tomatoes and tomato products	Reduce the risk of developing some cancers, especially prostate cancer
Dark green leafy vegetables, e.g. spinach	Reduce the risk of developing serious eye illnesses that may lead to blindness
Probiotics, e.g. live yogurt	Beneficial effects on the intestines and immune system

Check your understanding

1 Give two reasons why functional foods have increased in popularity. *(2 marks)*

2 State three functional foods and their role or benefit. An example has been provided for you: *(6 marks)*

   Functional food: garlic

   Role: lowers blood cholesterol levels

3 What is meant by the term 'functional food'? *(1 mark)*

7.1 Babies and children

Nutritional needs of groups

Revised

Our need for different nutrients changes throughout our life.

Meal planning should take into account the needs of different people, according to:

- their age
- their size
- their state of health
- their stage of development
- their daily physical activities.

Babies and children

Revised

Babies (birth–12 months)

- Should only have milk (preferably human breast milk) for first 4–6 months.
- Human breast milk is specially designed for human babies; it provides immunity and is easy to digest, but is low in **iron**.
- Babies are born with an iron store to last 3–4 months.
- If formula milk is used it must be made to the right concentration.
- After 4–6 months milk and small amounts of soft foods are given; this is **weaning**.
- New foods and larger portions should be **gradually introduced**.
- Foods that are known to cause **allergies** in some people should be very gradually introduced after the baby is at least 12 months old.
- Meals should be balanced.
- Babies do not need added sugar or salt in their food.

Young pre-school (1–4 years)

Dietary needs:

- Child is growing rapidly and physically active.
- Needs regular small meals and drinks; cannot eat large amounts of food in one go.
- The eatwell plate guidelines do not apply fully to this age group as a low fat and high fibre diet would not give them enough energy.
- They need protein for growth.
- They need fat for energy and vitamins A, D, E and K for development of brain and nervous system.
- They should be given whole milk not semi-skimmed or skimmed.
- They need carbohydrate for energy, preferably complex carbohydrates (potatoes, rice, bread).
- Calcium and vitamin D are needed for bone and teeth development.

> **Exam tip**
>
> Remember that the eatwell plate and dietary guidelines do not apply in full to these age groups as they would not receive all the nutrients they need, especially energy.

↑ **Figure 7.1**

- Iron and vitamin C are needed to produce enough energy.
- They need B vitamins to produce enough energy and maintain health of nervous system and muscles.

Guidance for feeding children at this age:

- Introduce new foods to expand the range eaten.
- Include fresh and raw foods.
- Sit at table to eat to encourage meal enjoyment; invite friends to share meals.
- Give child water to drink, not sweet drinks.
- Serve small portions; eat until they are full rather than eating everything on their plates (helps them recognise what their body tells them).
- Limit sweets, crisps, biscuits and snacks.
- Involve child in the whole process of eating (including shopping, cooking); teach them where foods come from and how to prepare and cook them.
- Make food fun.
- Provide choice.

School-aged children (5–12 years)

- A good variety and balance of nutrients is needed.
- Growth spurts require more good food containing protein and minerals for bone growth.
- Encourage children to try new foods.
- This is the ideal age to teach them more about food and how to prepare and cook it.
- From 5 years, follow the dietary guidelines and eatwell plate.
- Many children become inactive and an increasing number become overweight or obese.
- They should be discouraged from 'grazing' and 'snacking' during the day to avoid taking in too much energy from food which is then turned into fat.

Check your understanding `Tested`

1 Up to 6 months of age babies should only consume milk. What type of milk would be suitable for a baby of this age? *(1 mark)*

2 Identify two foods that should not be given to a baby until they are at least 12 months of age. *(2 marks)*

3 What is the main function of protein for pre-school children? *(1 mark)*

7.2 Teenagers

Key facts

Facts about teenagers	Meeting the dietary needs
Body changing from child to adult	• follow eatwell dietary guidelines • eat foods containing sufficient energy, protein, vitamins A, B group, C and D to enable bones, muscles and internal organs to grow properly
Growth spurts mean the need for food increases	Eat regular, well-balanced and filling meals
Tendency to sleep less and pressures of growth and school work can lead to tiredness and possible anaemia	Eat regular meals containing energy, iron and vitamin C
Skeleton should lay down most minerals during this age in order to reach **peak bone mass** when older	• regularly eat foods containing **calcium** and **vitamin D**, e.g. milk, yogurt, green leafy vegetables, bread, nuts and seeds • avoid drinking lots of carbonated (fizzy) drinks because phosphoric acid in them may affect the rate of bone mineralisation • take regular **load bearing exercise** (e.g. running, ball games) to stimulate bone mineralisation
Most growth occurs during sleep, so nutrients used for this must be replaced	Eat breakfast, particularly **protein-rich** foods (e.g. milk, egg, yogurt)
Breakfast can also aid concentration at school	Eat **wholegrain cereals** in bread, porridge and some breakfast cereals because they **release glucose slowly** and gradually into the bloodstream to help **maintain concentration**
Eating processed, fast and snack foods provides a lot of salt and concentrated energy from sugar and fat with few other nutrients This can lead to weight gain and diet-related diseases such as heart disease and diabetes	• eat **regular meals** containing a **wide variety of fresh foods**, especially fruit, vegetables and salads to provide a range of nutrients • limit intake of processed, fast and snack foods • drink plenty of **fresh water** • keep **physically active**

Exam tip

The teenage years are a period of rapid change and growth. Be aware of the problems faced by teenagers trying to eat a healthy diet and be able to explain how these problems can be overcome both at home and at school. For example, teenagers need to drink at least 2 litres of water per day, a school could help with this by providing free water at breaks and lunch but also ensuring there is access to water fountains around the school.

Teenage girls

Blood losses during menstruation (periods) may make teenage girls become anaemic.

They should regularly eat foods containing **iron** (e.g. red meat, wholegrain cereals, bread, lentils, dried apricots and dark green leafy vegetables) and **vitamin C** (e.g. kiwi fruit, peppers, new potatoes, guavas, dark green leafy vegetables and bean sprouts). The vitamin C helps the body absorb iron.

Teenage boys

Between 15 and 20 years, a significant amount of muscle grows in the arms, legs, chest and abdomen of teenage boys.

They need to eat sufficient **protein** (e.g. meat, fish, milk, yogurt, eggs, beans, lentils and cereal products) to encourage muscle growth.

Check your understanding
Tested ☐

1 Name two nutrients a girl will require more of during her teenage years. *(2 marks)*

2 State which nutrient should be eaten with iron to help its absorption. *(1 mark)*

3 Identify one good source of protein for a teenager. *(1 mark)*

4 Name two sources of calcium suitable for a packed lunch. *(2 marks)*

Nutritional needs of groups

7.3 Adults and senior citizens

Key facts

Facts about adults	Dietary needs
Body growth stops, so diet must maintain health and prevent diet-related diseases	Follow **current dietary guidelines**
Change in metabolic rate gradually slows down	Limit the amount of energy-dense foods that are eaten
Weight gain may occur due to the metabolic rate	Take regular physical exercise to control weight
Skeleton gradually starts to lose minerals	<ul><li>regularly eat foods containing **calcium** and **vitamin D**, e.g. milk, yogurt, green leafy vegetables, bread, seeds</li><li>take regular **load bearing exercise** (e.g. running, dancing) to maintain bone and muscle strength and to limit the rate of bone de-mineralisation</li></ul>
Women continue to menstruate until the menopause	<ul><li>regularly eat foods containing **iron** (e.g. red meat, bread, black treacle, dried apricots, dark green leafy vegetables) and **vitamin C** (e.g. kiwi fruit, new potatoes, Brussels sprouts, dark green leafy vegetables, bean sprouts)</li><li>vitamin C helps the body absorb iron</li></ul>

Facts about senior citizens (elderly people)	Dietary needs
Systems in the body slow down, e.g. digestive and circulatory (blood) systems	<ul><li>eat plenty of fibre (NSP) to prevent constipation and diverticular disease</li><li>drink plenty of water to prevent constipation and help the kidneys to work properly</li></ul>
Absorption of nutrients may not be as efficient as before. This can lead to **anaemia** or to early signs of **scurvy** (lack of vitamin C)	<ul><li>regularly eat foods containing sufficient **iron** (e.g. red meat, wholegrain cereals, lentils, some curry spices, dark green leafy vegetables) and **vitamin C** (e.g. citrus fruits, peppers, new potatoes, guavas, Brussels sprouts)</li></ul>
<ul><li>bones naturally lose minerals and become weakened (**osteoporosis**)</li><li>some parts of the body wear out, e.g. joints</li></ul>	<ul><li>regularly eat foods containing **calcium** and **vitamin D**, e.g. milk, cheese, green leafy vegetables, bones of canned fish, nuts</li><li>take regular **load bearing exercise** (e.g. walking, dancing) to maintain bone and muscle strength, limit the rate of bone de-mineralisation and stimulate the bones to take up calcium</li></ul>
Living indoors most of the time may mean limited exposure to **sunlight** to make **vitamin D**	<ul><li>vitamin D supplements recommended for people over 65 years</li><li>expose the skin to regular doses of **sunlight**</li></ul>
Metabolic rate gradually slows down	Limit the amount of energy-dense foods that are eaten
Weight gain may occur due to the metabolic rate	Take regular physical exercise to control weight
Appetite may get **smaller**	May need small, regular energy-dense meals to maintain energy intake
Eyesight becomes **weaker**	Eat foods containing antioxidants vitamins A, C and E to help prevent age-related eye conditions
Blood pressure may **increase**	<ul><li>limit sodium/salt intake</li><li>limit intake of ready meals, which may have a high sodium/salt content</li></ul>
Sense of **smell** and **taste** may **weaken**	Avoid adding extra salt to compensate – try other flavours, e.g. herbs and spices
Memory loss may occur	This may be due to vitamin B_{12} deficiency – B_{12} is found in liver, shellfish, red meat, milk and fortified breakfast cereals; a B_{12} supplement may be needed

Possible problems for senior citizens preparing, cooking and eating food

Oral (mouth) – chewing and swallowing problems may be caused by:

- loss of teeth, false teeth or gum disease
- effects of stroke or disease, e.g. Parkinson's disease.

Manual dexterity – problems using the hands may be caused by:

- arthritis, causing painful, swollen fingers
- frail skin, easily cut or burnt
- stroke or Parkinson's disease, making holding things difficult.

Social:

- may lose interest in food due to loneliness, isolation, being widowed, loss of independence, living in a care home, ill health, depression
- may not be able to cook for themselves (lack of skills, lack of facilities)
- difficulty buying and carrying food from the shops (walking difficulties, lack of transport, disability, distance to shops).

Poverty: limited amount to spend on food.

Effects of medicines: some medicines affect how nutrients are absorbed and affect the taste of food.

Changes to senses: loss of smell and taste may make appetite smaller.

Help available for senior citizens

- Lunch clubs – hot meals provided in social setting for a small price.
- Mobility buses – for shopping or outings to clubs.
- Meals on wheels – meals (ready-to-eat or frozen) delivered to their homes.
- Food co-operatives – bring food for sale to an area in a van.
- Home helps – people who can help with shopping and cooking.

> **Exam tip**
>
> Questions related to elderly people tend to focus on problems associated with healthy eating and how these problems could be overcome, or nutrient differences compared to other age groups. For example, as we age we have a reduced capacity to absorb nutrients such as iron, which can cause anaemia. Therefore, elderly people must have enough iron-rich foods in their diet such as red meat, eggs, dark green leafy vegetables. They must also eat enough vitamin C to help absorb the iron, to maximise absorption.

Check your understanding

Tested

1 Give one reason an elderly person may need to take a vitamin D supplement. *(1 mark)*

2 Elderly people should increase their energy intake. True or false? *(1 mark)*

3 Describe three reasons why an elderly person may not eat a balanced diet. *(6 marks)*

4 Identify two nutrients important to maintaining the health of a person's bones. *(2 marks)*

7.4 Pregnant women

Key facts   Revised

Facts about pregnancy	Dietary needs
Food is needed to maintain the mother's body and for the growing **foetus (baby)**, but not enough food for two adults	<ul><li>follow the current dietary guidelines</li><li>eat foods containing sufficient energy, protein, vitamins A, B group, C, D to maintain mother's body and enable the bones, muscles and internal organs of the baby to grow properly</li><li>eat regular, balanced meals</li></ul>
<ul><li>the skeleton of the baby gradually changes from **cartilage** to bone as it **mineralises**</li><li>the baby gets calcium from the mother's blood supply</li><li>if the mother's diet lacks calcium and vitamin D the baby will take calcium from the mother's bones, which will weaken them</li><li>young pregnant women must have enough calcium to mineralise their own bones as well as the baby's</li></ul>	<ul><li>regularly eat foods containing **calcium** and **vitamin D** (except liver as it contains too much vitamin A), e.g. milk, yogurt, green leafy vegetables, bread, nuts</li><li>avoid drinking lots of carbonated (fizzy) drinks because phosphoric acid in them may affect the rate of bone mineralisation</li><li>take regular **load bearing exercise** (e.g. walking, gentle running, dancing) to stimulate bone mineralisation</li><li>avoid alcohol, caffeine and nicotine, which prevent calcium being properly taken up in the skeleton</li></ul>
<ul><li>the volume of the mother's blood increases by 50%</li><li>in the last 3 months of pregnancy, the baby must build up a store of iron to last it throughout the first 3–4 months after birth</li></ul>	<ul><li>regularly eat foods containing **iron** (e.g. red meat, wholegrain cereals, bread, lentils, dried apricots, molasses) and **vitamin C** (e.g. citrus fruits, peppers, new potatoes, dark green leafy vegetables, Brussels sprouts)</li><li>vitamin C helps the body absorb iron</li><li>iron supplements may be needed to prevent anaemia</li></ul>
<ul><li>the unborn baby can develop disabling defects in the spine, e.g. spina bifida; research shows that if the mother has a lack of folate (vitamin B$_9$) in her diet, her baby may be at greater risk of developing spinal defects</li></ul>	<ul><li>if possible, take a **folate** supplement before becoming pregnant and for the first 12 weeks of pregnancy</li><li>eat plenty of foods containing folate (e.g. potatoes, fruits, asparagus, okra, beans and seeds, fortified breakfast cereals)</li></ul>
<ul><li>pregnancy hormones slow down the muscles in the intestines; this can lead to constipation</li></ul>	<ul><li>eat plenty of **fibre (NSP)** to prevent constipation and diverticular disease</li><li>drink plenty of **water** to prevent constipation and help the kidneys work properly</li></ul>
<ul><li>weight gain should be regular and carefully monitored</li><li>fat is stored in the pregnant woman's body to provide energy for breastfeeding</li></ul>	<ul><li>limit the amount of energy-dense foods that are eaten</li><li>take regular physical exercise to control weight</li></ul>

Foods to avoid during pregnancy

Pregnant women need to avoid foods that may either cause food poisoning or contain too much of a nutrient which could harm their growing baby. These are:

- pâtés, soft cheeses, e.g. Brie, Camembert, Chevre (goat's cheese) – may contain Listeria bacteria

- soft blue cheeses and cheeses made with unpasteurised milk

- raw or lightly cooked meat, especially products made with minced beef (e.g. burgers) – these should be cooked right through to at least 70°C in the middle

- liver, liver products and vitamin A supplements (e.g. cod liver oil)

- raw or partly cooked eggs – may contain Salmonella bacteria

- some types of fish, e.g. tuna, swordfish – may contain mercury, which may affect the baby's brain and nervous system
- alcohol and caffeine – may cause baby to be underweight.

Lactation (breastfeeding)

Weight gained during pregnancy will be gradually lost as fat stores are used to produce milk. Breastfeeding women are advised to:

- eat a balanced diet. Energy needs will increase, but some of this comes from the fat stores built up in pregnancy
- eat foods containing iron and vitamin C to make up for blood losses during childbirth
- eat foods containing calcium and vitamin D to provide for the baby's growing skeleton and maintenance of the mother's skeleton
- eat foods containing protein to enable milk to be made and to help the mother's body recover from the birth
- drink plenty of fluid to allow milk to be produced
- keep physically active.

Check your understanding   Tested

1 Give one reason why a woman planning to have a baby should increase her intake of folate.   *(1 mark)*

2 Identify three foods that should be avoided during pregnancy.   *(3 marks)*

3 Explain why those three foods (from above) should be avoided during pregnancy.   *(6 marks)*

7.5 People trying to lose weight

Key facts

Being overweight or obese:

- makes people likely to develop:
  - heart disease
  - diabetes
  - high blood pressure
  - osteoarthritis in the hips and knees.
- makes people feel depressed about their looks
- is a risk factor if a person needs surgery
- leads to breathing problems because of fat on the chest
- causes skin infections because bacteria are trapped under fat folds.

People put on weight because

- over a period of time they take in more energy from food than they use in physical exercise
- they change their eating habits, e.g. they eat more energy-dense processed, fast and snack foods
- they eat between meals (snacking and grazing)
- they have a less active (sedentary) job
- they do not take physical exercise and spend a lot of time sitting and being inactive.

Losing weight permanently

- takes a long time
- takes motivation, determination and support from friends and family
- requires someone to use more energy in a day than they take in from food so that fat stores in their body are used up
- requires someone to gradually and permanently change their eating habits.

> **Exam tip**
>
> Questions on this topic often cover meal or diet adaptation and healthy eating. Be prepared to suggest some ideas and reasons for changing a given diet. For example, if someone does not currently eat breakfast but at 9 a.m. eats a large slice of cake and a milkshake, you could suggest that they eat a breakfast consisting of poached eggs on seeded bread with a cup of tea in the morning. The eggs would provide them with protein, which is filling, so is likely to reduce the chance of snacking later in the day, so may reduce the overall energy/fat intake, which will help them to lose weight in the long term.

Changing eating habits and behaviours

● Eat fewer **energy-dense foods**, e.g. crisps, biscuits, cakes, fried foods, pizzas, mayonnaise and sweet milky drinks such as café lattes.

● Eat more **low energy foods,** e.g. fruit, salads, wholegrain cereals.

● Eat more **low fat or low sugar versions** of foods, such as cheese, spreads, sweetened drinks, yogurts.

● Change **methods of cooking** – grill, steam, bake rather than fry.

● Change **food portions** – try using a smaller plate and resist second helpings.

● Increase **physical activity,** e.g. walking, cycling, running, swimming, climbing stairs, playing a sport.

Check your understanding   Tested

1   Identify three health or social problems associated with being overweight or obese.   *(3 marks)*

2   Identify four reasons people gain weight.   *(4 marks)*

3   Identify four lifestyle changes someone could make to help them lose weight.   *(4 marks)*

7.6 Vegetarians

Key facts

A vegetarian diet

● is based mostly on plant foods

● does not include foods or food products where an animal, bird or fish has had to be killed.

Reasons for following a vegetarian diet

● Do not want to eat flesh from dead animals, birds or fish.

● Disagree with raising and killing animals, birds or fish for food (consider it to be cruel, a waste of land, water, energy, food).

● Consider a vegetarian diet to be healthier than a meat-eating diet.

● Religious reasons.

Types of vegetarians

● **Lacto–ovo vegetarian** – eat animal products, e.g. eggs (**ovo**), milk (**lacto**), that have not required a bird or animal to be killed or suffer physically.

● **Lacto vegetarian** – as above, but will not eat eggs.

● **Vegans (strict vegetarians)** – do not eat **any** animal food products; only eat plant foods.

> **Exam tip**
>
> Have an understanding of the different types of vegetarian, including what they do and do not eat. Think about how a vegetarian or vegan could consume a balanced diet.

↑ Figure 7.2

↑ Figure 7.3

Food labelling helps vegetarians to identify suitable and unsuitable foods. Examples of symbols used are shown in Figures 7.2 and 7.3.

Dietary and nutritional needs

Follow current dietary guidelines.

It is particularly important to include enough iron, vitamin C, protein and vitamin B_{12}.

Iron:

● Iron from plant foods is less easily absorbed by the body.

● Plant sources of iron: wholegrain cereals and cereal products, bread (added by law), fortified breakfast cereals, lentils and beans, dried apricots and figs, nuts, seeds, some curry spices, black treacle, green leafy vegetables, okra, broccoli, peas, Brussels sprouts, cocoa and dark plain chocolate, molasses.

- If the need for iron is high (e.g. after loss of blood or due to heavy periods), a vegetarian iron supplement may be needed, e.g. blackstrap molasses capsules.

Vitamin C helps the body to absorb iron.

Protein:

- HBV proteins mostly found in animal foods except soya beans and quinoa.
- Lacto and lacto–ovo vegetarians can gain enough protein from animal products.
- A combination of LBV plant proteins should be eaten to provide all essential amino acids (**protein complementing**) – this is very important for vegans.
- Soya milk and soya products are available, e.g. desserts, yogurts, drinks, tofu, tempeh, custards.
- Quorn® is man-made from a **mycoprotein**. It is made into meat substitute products such as burgers and sausages. It is unsuitable for vegans because Quorn® is grown on egg protein and may contain milk.
- Protein complementing:
  - lentil soup and bread
  - nut, seed and bread roast
  - nut stir-fry and egg-free pasta
  - vegetable and soya bean curry, and brown rice and naan bread
  - hummus and bread.

Vitamin B$_{12}$:

- Mainly found in animal foods.
- Found in dairy products and eggs – lacto and lacto–ovo vegetarians should ensure they get enough.
- Found in yeast extract, soya milks, sunflower margarine and fortified breakfast cereals.
- Vegans may need to take a supplement.

↑ **Figure 7.4 Protein complementing: hummus and bread**

Check your understanding

Tested

1 Give three reasons why someone may choose to follow a vegetarian diet. *(3 marks)*

2 Identify two sources of protein suitable for a vegetarian. *(2 marks)*

3 Identify one good food source of vitamin B$_{12}$ suitable for a vegan. *(1 mark)*

7.7–7.8 Coeliacs and diabetics

Coeliacs

- Coeliac disease is caused by intolerance to **gluten**.
- Gluten is the protein in wheat, barley and rye and products made from them. Some people are also sensitive to oats, as the protein in oats is similar to that in gluten.
- The gut damage caused by coeliac disease prevents other nutrients from being absorbed in the small intestine.
- A lifelong condition.
- **Symptoms**:
  - weight loss (but not in all cases)
  - chronic lack of energy, and ongoing tiredness
  - chronic diarrhoea
  - anaemia – due to poor absorption of iron
  - poor growth in children
  - other nutritional deficiencies

Food labelling helps coeliacs to identify suitable and unsuitable foods. Examples of symbols used are shown here.

↑ **Figure 7.5 Reproduced with the permission of Coeliac UK**

↑ **Figure 7.6 Examples of manufacturers' own labelling**

Foods that coeliacs **can** eat: agar, almonds, amaranth, buckwheat, carrageenan, cassava (manioc/tapioca), chestnuts, corn (maize), linseeds (flax), gram flour*, millet, polenta, potato flour, peas, beans, lentils, quinoa, rice, sago, sorghum, soya flour*, urd/urid (lentil flour)*. Those marked * and alternative flours need to be checked for their gluten status, as contamination with grains containing gluten can happen when the flour is milled.

> **Exam tip**
>
> Be prepared to be given a recipe and identify what ingredient(s) make the recipe unsuitable for a coeliac. For example, pancakes made with wheat flour would not be suitable; however you could substitute the wheat flour for gluten-free almond flour.

Diabetics

- Diabetes is a health condition where the amount of **glucose** in the blood is too high.
- Blood glucose is controlled by the hormone **insulin**.
- Insulin is like a key, it 'unlocks' body cells to let glucose in.
- Diabetics either don't produce enough insulin or their body is unable to use it.
- **Hypoglycaemia** means low blood glucose.
- **Hyperglycaemia** means high blood glucose (damages blood vessels in eyes, hands, feet, kidneys, etc.).

- Diabetics are more likely to develop high blood pressure, heart disease, strokes.
- No cure, but diabetes can be managed to control symptoms and limit long-term damage.

Exam tip

There are two types of diabetes, Type 1 and Type 2. Type 1 is insulin dependent diabetes, which is mainly managed by insulin injections. You should be aware of this type of diabetes but the questions in the exam will focus on Type 2 diabetes.

Two types of diabetes

Type 1	Type 2
- insulin dependent (need regular daily injections) - develops in childhood or early adulthood - immune system destroys insulin-producing cells in the pancreas - need to eat a balanced diet (eatwell plate) - need to test blood and/or urine for sugar levels	- non-insulin dependent - body does not produce enough insulin or insulin does not work properly - linked to people being overweight or obese - treated (and development prevented) by: balanced diet (some people have to have tablets or injections as well), increasing physical exercise, losing weight

There has been a large increase in the numbers of people developing Type 2 diabetes, including many young people.

Symptoms of diabetes

- weight loss (particularly in Type 1)
- lack of energy, tiredness
- thirst
- need to urinate more often
- blurred vision
- genital itching.

Dietary advice for diabetics

- follow current dietary guidelines
- limit sugar intake
- eat complex carbohydrate foods to release glucose slowly into the body, so it does less damage and the body has time to deal with it
- no need to buy specially made diabetic foods
- control intake of fat and salt to help prevent heart disease and high blood pressure
- increase fruit and vegetable intake to provide antioxidants
- read food labels to become aware of what different foods contain; look for 'hidden' sugars and chemical names of sugars, e.g. sucrose, dextrose, maltodextrin, glucose syrup.

Check your understanding　　　　　　　　　　　　　　　　Tested

1. Identify one alternative to wheat flour that would be suitable for a coeliac. *(1 mark)*

2. State two symptoms associated with gluten intolerance. *(2 marks)*

3. Hypoglycaemia means a low level of blood glucose. True or false? *(1 mark)*

4. Explain three dietary guidelines that a diabetic (Type 2) could follow to help control their diabetes. *(6 marks)*

5. Give one reason why a diabetic is encouraged to read food labels when buying food. *(1 mark)*

7.9 Food allergies and intolerances

Nutritional needs of groups

Key facts

- A **food allergy** means an allergic (bad) reaction to a food or ingredient.

- An **allergen** is a substance in food that causes an allergy.

- Allergens make the body produce **histamine**, which causes these symptoms in a few seconds, minutes or hours:

  - skin rashes

  - itchy skin and eyes

  - runny nose

  - swollen lips, eyelids, face

  - wheezing, coughing

  - anaphylactic shock.

- **Anaphylactic shock** is a very sudden and very serious allergic reaction:

  - mouth and throat swells

  - cannot swallow, speak or breathe properly

  - can be fatal

  - must be treated very quickly.

- **Foods that cause reactions** in some people include eggs, peanuts, other nuts, seeds, strawberries, kiwi fruit, seafood, e.g. prawns and shrimps (there are others).

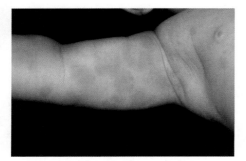

↑ **Figure 7.7 This child has had an allergic reaction to a food**

Food intolerance

- Sometimes called **food sensitivity**.

- **Symptoms**:

  - pain and bloating in the abdomen

  - diarrhoea

  - nausea (feeling sick)

  - muscle and joint aches and pains

  - general tiredness and weakness.

- Hard to diagnose.

- An example is **lactose intolerance** – cannot digest **lactose** in milk and dairy products. Bacteria in the gut break it down and cause the symptoms. Avoid all foods containing milk, milk products, lactose, and eat lactose-free products.

- Other intolerances – chocolate, cheese, some food additives, wheat gluten (but not always full coeliac disease).

Exam tip

This topic links well to Topic 7.7 (coeliacs), as you may be asked in the exam to adapt a recipe to avoid a food intolerance or allergy.

Managing allergies and intolerances

- Eat a balanced diet.

- Avoid known problem foods.

- People likely to have anaphylactic shock should carry an **epipen**, to inject into their arm or leg if they have a reaction. An epipen injects **adrenaline** into the blood to control the symptoms while the person goes to hospital for further urgent medical treatment.

- Read food labels carefully.

- Well known allergens are usually shown on food labels.

- Beware of 'hidden' names, e.g. peanuts are also called ground nuts (e.g. ground nut oil); 'arachis' is the Latin name for peanuts and might be an ingredient in medicines.

- Check restaurant menus by asking about ingredients used if eating out.

- Tell other people about your allergy so they understand and can help if needed.

- Most food companies will provide a list of products containing possible allergic ingredients.

INGREDIENTS Wholegrain Oats (88%), Sunflower Oil, Sustainable Palm Fruit Oil, Sea Salt, Raising Agent: Sodium Bicarbonate.

ALLERGY ADVICE: Contains Gluten. Both our recipe and factory are nut free. We cannot guarantee that our ingredients are nut free. Manufactured on equipment that handles milk.

↑ **Figure 7.8** Allergy advice

Check your understanding   Tested

1 What is meant by the term 'food allergy'?   *(1 mark)*

2 Identify three foods that people may be allergic to.   *(3 marks)*

3 What is meant by the term 'food intolerance'?   *(1 mark)*

7.10 Coronary heart disease (CHD)

Key facts

- CHD is a disease where the **coronary arteries** (which give the heart oxygen) become blocked.
- Risk factors:
  - **high cholesterol** in the blood
  - **smoking cigarettes** – makes the blood sticky so more likely to form blockages
  - **high blood pressure** – strains the heart and arteries; may be caused by eating too much **salt**
  - being **overweight** or **obese**
  - **lack of exercise** – the heart needs to be exercised to keep it healthy.

Cholesterol

- Made in the liver from fats in the food we eat.
- Eating a lot of **saturated fats** (in meat, cheese, butter, suet, lard and solid vegetable fats) makes more cholesterol. Sometimes called 'bad' cholesterol.
- Eating more **unsaturated fats** (in vegetable, nut and seed oils) makes less cholesterol. Sometimes called 'good' cholesterol.

Dietary advice to prevent CHD

- Follow current dietary guidelines.
- Eat fruit and vegetables – **antioxidants** and **fibre** in them help prevent damage to arteries by keeping cholesterol low and preventing other substances from damaging them.
- Choose low fat foods.
- Limit saturated fat intake.
- Grill or bake foods, rather than fry.
- Trim fat off foods.
- Reduce amount of fat spread on foods.
- Reduce salt intake – use other flavours, eat fewer salty snacks, ready meals and baked items that contain baking powder (baking powder contains sodium).

Other advice

- Do not start smoking; stop smoking if already a smoker.
- Take more physical exercise.
- Try to lose weight if necessary.

> **Exam tip**
>
> This is a nutrition exam so you are not expected to know the detail of how coronary heart disease occurs, but you do need to understand the basic risk factors and how these could be avoided. Remember to make links to healthy eating and dietary guidelines in your answers.

Check your understanding

1 Identify three factors that increase the risk of coronary heart disease. *(3 marks)*
2 Describe three ways to lower the risk of developing coronary heart disease. *(6 marks)*

8.1 Social and economic diversity

Key facts

Factors that influence our food choices:

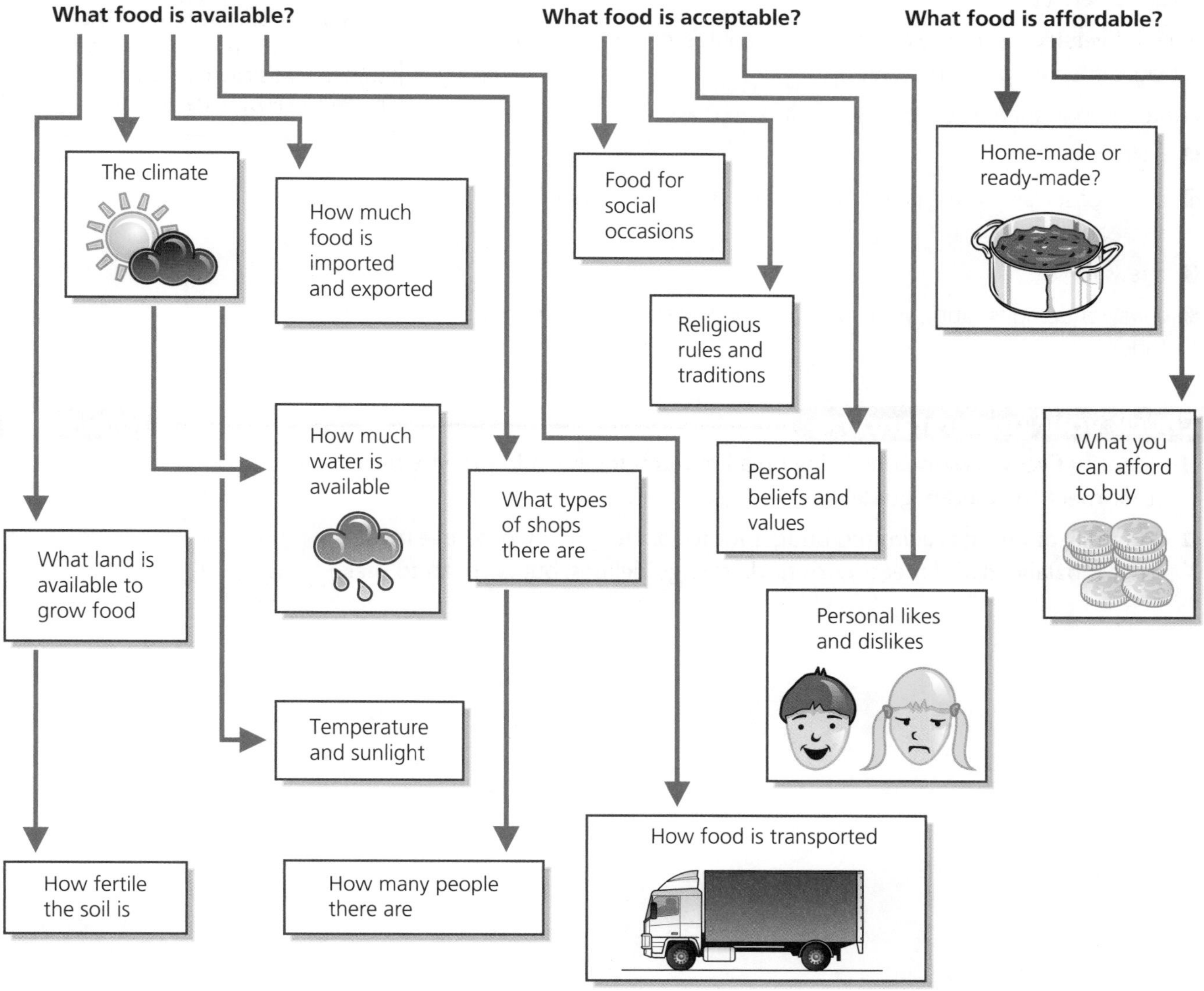

↑ Figure 8.1

Social and economic diversity

Economic diversity:

- **Economic diversity** means the different amounts of money that different people live on and can afford to spend on food.

- Rent, gas, electricity and other bills must be paid. People with a limited income may have to spend less on food in order to pay for these.

- Cheaper food products are often made with cheap ingredients, such as sugar, fats, salt.

Saving money on a limited income:

- Use cheaper cuts of meat, e.g. shin of beef, which may need longer to cook.

- Use alternative, cheaper proteins, e.g. peas, beans, lentils, instead of meat or to make meat go further.

- Make your own food rather than buying ready-made – cook a large batch and freeze some.
- Use foods in season, e.g. fruits and vegetables.
- Make use of special offers, and collect and use money-off vouchers.
- Use supermarket own brands and 'value' line products.

Social diversity:

Social diversity means the differences in people's interests, opinions, activities, friendship groups, values.

Food is important in social diversity as it is used as:

- a gift
- a way of socialising, e.g. going out for a meal, sharing a drink with someone
- a reward
- a way of demonstrating your status, e.g. buying expensive wines or foods.

Check your understanding   Tested

1 Identify five ways someone living on a limited budget could prepare meals that meet the dietary guidelines.   *(5 marks)*

2 A family of four has a limited budget for food. Design a two-course meal that is balanced and meets current dietary guidelines, but is cheap to make.   *(4 marks)*

8.2 Cultural and religious diversity

Culture

Culture is:

- ways of life and behaviour
- what we know and believe
- customs, habits, laws, morals
- inheritance and traditions
- part of normal behaviour, e.g. eating certain foods
- a person's values, e.g. their perception of good and bad foods, good and bad behaviour.

Food culture

Food reinforces bonds between people and is an important part of celebrations.

Food culture is how, what, why, when and where people choose to eat.

How food culture has changed

What has changed	What people used to do	How it has changed	Effects of these changes
Where food comes from	Home grown food and small local shops	Food comes from large shops	Lack of knowledge about food
How we buy food	Buy food every day	Buy food once a week or month	• fewer small shops • foods have a long shelf-life
How we prepare food	Women cooked fresh foods at home	• ready meals eaten • more women at work • less time for cooking	• fewer people have cooking skills • many convenience foods available • not just women cooking
What we eat	• traditional meals • limited or seasonal choices, few food imports • little packaging used	• snack, fast and ready-made foods • travel has widened food experiences • more types of foods available, many imported • much packaging used	• many energy-dense foods and not enough fruits or vegetables eaten • many foods highly coloured and flavoured • food from other cultures very popular • many foods eaten out of season (imported) – consider energy use and environmental damage
Where we eat	Most food eaten at home	Food often eaten outside the home or alone in front of the TV	• eating out is a normal part of culture • catering industry very large • family meals are less common
When we eat	• mostly at regular set meal times • food shops opened 6 days a week during the day only	• people eat at different times in one home • food can be purchased at any time	• easy to overeat • snacking may lead to weight gain

Religion

Most religions have dietary rules or laws, often within traditional celebrations.

Religious faith	Dietary rules
Buddhism	• mostly vegetarian; some avoid meat and dairy products • Buddhist monks fast and can only obtain food through donation by believers
Christianity	• fasting is sometimes observed • before Easter, certain foods are given up for 40 days and nights (Lent) • Christmas food celebrations for the birth of Jesus
Hinduism	• do not eat beef or pork • avoid foods that cause pain to animals; vegetarianism is encouraged • believe food contains energies that are absorbed by people • onions, garlic and alcohol may be avoided because they affect spiritualism • dairy foods are believed to enhance spiritual purity • sometimes fast
Islam	• halal food is lawful, e.g. meat and poultry slaughtered in a ritual called zibah • rules set out in Qur'an • haram foods are unlawful, e.g. pork and pork products (e.g. gelatine), alcohol, foods with emulsifiers made from animal fats, frozen vegetables with sauce, some margarines, drinks with caffeine, breads with dried yeast • fast for a month during daylight hours during Ramadan. Not allowed liquids either • Eid is the festival at end of Ramadan
Judaism	• kashrut are Jewish food laws • kosher foods are allowed – fish (with scales and fins), animals that chew the cud and have cloven (split) hooves, e.g. cows, sheep • trefah foods are not allowed, e.g. pork, shellfish • dairy foods and meat must not be prepared in the same cooking area or using the same equipment • no work is allowed on Saturdays; food is prepared and cooked the day before, e.g. slow-cooked stew • on Yom Kippur (Day of Atonement) Jews fast from dusk to dusk • feast days include Rosh Hashanah and Passover
Rastafarianism	• eat strictly according to I-tal; food must be natural and clean • do not eat pork or fish longer than 30cm • eat many fruits and vegetables • cook with coconut oil • do not drink alcohol, milk or coffee, but drink herbal teas
Sikhism	• many are vegetarian • on special days foods are eaten in the temple • eat together to show they are equal • some do not drink alcohol, tea or coffee

Check your understanding   Tested

1   Explain four changes that have occurred in the last 25 years in relation to
    the way we buy, prepare and eat food.   *(8 marks)*

2   Identify two religions where vegetarianism is encouraged.   *(2 marks)*

9.1 The transfer of heat to foods

Key facts

Food is cooked

- to destroy harmful bacteria and help prevent food poisoning
- to develop the flavour of foods
- to make food easier to bite, chew, swallow, digest
- to make foods more appealing and attractive to eat
- to give a variety by using different cooking methods
- to provide hot food
- to destroy natural toxins (poisons) in some foods
- to enable foods to rise, thicken, dissolve, set.

The transfer of heat to foods

- Heat is energy.
- Foods are made up of atoms joined together as molecules.
- Molecules receive energy and vibrate and move quickly.
- Heat is produced – the quicker the movement, the more heat.
- **Conduction** means heat passed through solid materials, e.g. metals, food.
- **Convection** means heat passed through liquid or gas.
- **Radiation** means heat passed through space (not through solid, liquid or gas).

> **Exam tip**
>
> This topic is commonly asked in exams, make sure you learn it and have some examples of heat transfer too.

Conduction and convection

3.
- Heat from water passes into potatoes
- Potato molecules vibrate and produce heat by **conduction**
- Starch in potatoes cooks and softens

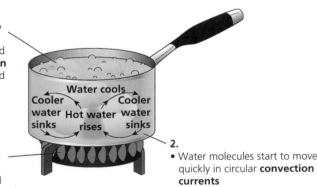

Water cools
Cooler water sinks
Hot water rises
Cooler water sinks

1.
- Energy from gas transferred to metal pan
- Metal molecules vibrate and produce heat
- Heat **conducted** into water

2.
- Water molecules start to move quickly in circular **convection currents**

↑ **Figure 9.1**

Radiation

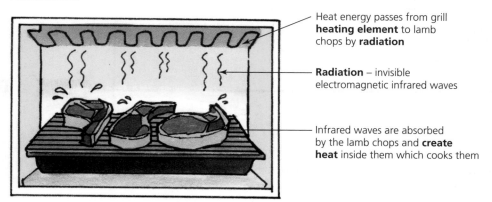

Heat energy passes from grill **heating element** to lamb chops by **radiation**

Radiation – invisible electromagnetic infrared waves

Infrared waves are absorbed by the lamb chops and **create heat** inside them which cooks them

⬆ Figure 9.2

Check your understanding

Tested

1 State three reasons why food is cooked. *(3 marks)*

2 Identify the three types of heat transfer. *(3 marks)*

3 Match the following methods of heat transfer to their descriptions. *(3 marks)*

Conduction The passing of heat through a gas or a liquid.

Convection The passing of heat through a space without the use of a solid, liquid or gas.

Radiation The passing of heat through solid materials such as metal or food.

9.2 Grilling, frying, roasting, baking and barbecuing

Grilling
Revised

- A fast cooking method.
- Heat transfer is radiation.
- **Fats** in food **melt** and **drain away** – this reduces the fat in food so is a healthier cooking method than frying.
- Food should be no more than **3.5cm thick** – if it is thicker, the outside may be overcooked by the time the inside is cooked.
- Meat cuts should be **tender**, e.g. steaks, chops.
- Grills are in electric and gas cookers, or special infrared grill, or combination microwave oven and grill.

> **Exam tip**
>
> Topic 9.2 makes strong links to methods of heat transfer and how to change cooking methods to make a food or dish meet healthy eating guidelines.

Frying
Revised

Key facts
- Frying means cooking food in hot fat or oil.
- **Deep frying** is frying in a pan or electric fryer with oil several centimetres deep.
- **Shallow frying** is frying in a frying pan or sauté pan with a little oil or fat.
- Heat transfer is conduction (from pan) and convection (from oil).
- Fried foods **soak up oil**, which **increases their fat content and energy density**.
- Remove excess oil after cooking using absorbent kitchen paper.

Dry frying
- Some foods, e.g. minced beef, can be dry fried.
- **No oil** is added to the pan.
- Heated gently to melt the **natural fat** present in the food.

Stir-frying
- Traditionally, food is cooked in a **wok**.
- The wok should be hot before cooking.
- Meat and poultry must be cooked thoroughly.
- A small amount of oil is used – stir-frying is a **healthy** cooking method.
- If the food becomes dry while stir-frying, add a little **water** to prevent it sticking rather than more oil.

↑ **Figure 9.3 Shallow frying**

Roasting
Revised

- Roasting is cooking food in a hot oven with a little oil.
- Heat transfer is mainly conduction from the roasting pan and bones in the meat or metal skewers placed in food.

- **Water evaporates** and causes **flavours** to become **concentrated**.
- Meat for roasting should be tender – tough cuts will not be tenderised.
- Meat and poultry must be cooked right through.
- **Spit roasting** is cooking food over an open fire or flames while turning it slowly.

It is important to choose the right type of joint for roasting:

Type of meat	Roasting joints
Poultry (chicken, turkey, duck, pheasant)	Whole bird, leg quarter, breast, turkey breast crown, poussin (very small chicken), drumstick, thigh
Lamb	Leg, shoulder, breast, best end of neck (crown roast), loin, neck fillet, chops
Pork	Leg, fillet, spare ribs, chops, belly, hand, shoulder
Bacon	Gammon, collar
Beef	Silverside, topside, sirloin, fore rib, ribs

Baking

Revised

- Baking means cooking food in a hot oven without oil.
- Heat transfer is convection and conduction.
- Heat causes foods to **rise and set**, e.g. cakes, scones, choux pastry, bread, Yorkshire puddings.
- Oven must be hot when foods are placed in it.
- If the oven door is opened, cold, heavy air will go into the oven and the baked goods may sink.

Barbecuing

Revised

- Foods are usually cooked outside over hot, glowing charcoal (or a gas barbecue).
- Heat transfer is radiation from the hot charcoal.
- Food picks up a smoked flavour.
- Turn food frequently for even cooking.
- Make sure outside does not cook too quickly, otherwise inside may be undercooked and cause food poisoning.
- Brush some foods, e.g. vegetables, fish, with an oily dressing to stop them becoming dry.

Check your understanding

Tested

1. State how heat is transferred when grilling. *(1 mark)*
2. Identify one reason why grilling is a healthier cooking method than frying. *(1 mark)*
3. State two reasons why some fish is deep fried in batter. *(2 marks)*
4. State two reasons why stir-frying is considered a healthy cooking method. *(2 marks)*
5. Explain four ways to reduce the risk of food poisoning when cooking on a barbecue (BBQ). *(8 marks)*

9.3 Boiling, poaching, simmering, steaming, stewing, braising and microwaving

Boiling, poaching, simmering and steaming

Revised

Boiling

- Foods cooked in boiling water (100°C) to tenderise them.
- Heat transfer is convection.
- Suitable foods include eggs, pasta, rice, vegetables, some joints of meat.
- Heat damages C and B group vitamins – conserve them by using a little water and serve immediately.

Poaching and simmering

- Gentle methods of cooking.
- Heat transfer is convection.
- Food cooked just below boiling point.
- **Simmering**: suitable foods include tough cuts of meat, vegetables, pasta, rice, pulses.
- **Poaching**: suitable foods include fish, eggs.

Steaming

- Gentle method of cooking.
- Heat transfer is mostly convection from steam.
- Food very **easy to eat and digest**; suitable for people who have been ill, infants, young children, elderly people, people with digestive problems.
- Food does not overcook or develop a crust.
- Fewer vitamins lost.
- Food can be steamed:
  - on a covered plate over a pan of boiling water
  - in a special steamer pan
  - in an electric steamer
  - in a plastic steamer in a microwave oven.

> **Exam tip**
>
> Questions on cooking methods are likely to focus on:
> - Types of food or dishes that can be cooked by a particular method.
> - The effect of the cooking method on the nutritional value of the food(s).
> - How you could make the cooking method healthier.
> - Why the food is cooked in this way, e.g. to tenderise meat or retain more vitamin C.
> - What happens to the food when it is cooked.

Stewing and braising

Revised

Stewing

- Gentle, slow cooking method.
- Suitable for foods that need to be tenderised, e.g. tough meat cuts, poultry, hard fruits (apples), pulses (beans).
- Food usually stewed in a covered pan on the hob or a heat-proof covered dish in the oven.
- Heat transfer is conduction and convection.

- Food cooked with a liquid (water, stock or wine) and other ingredients, e.g. vegetables.
- Cooked on low heat for several hours.
- The liquid tenderises the food and flavours develop – all served together.
- Meat becomes tender because stewing changes **collagen (protein)** to **gelatine (protein)**.
- **Electric slow cookers** – cook food slowly. Save fuel and thermostatically controlled.

Braising

- Similar to stewing but less liquid is used.
- Food is placed on a bed of other ingredients, e.g. vegetables and liquid.
- Covered and cooked in the oven for several hours until tender.
- If meat is cooked this way on the hob it is called a **pot roast**.

Microwaving

Revised

- Used to cook a wide range of foods.
- Uses little electricity and takes up little space.
- Heat transfer is radiation (microwaves) and some conduction (from vibrating food molecules).
- Easy to overcook foods.
- Less chance of vitamins being destroyed.
- Foods do not develop a crust.
- Some models have a combination grill and convection oven to complete the cooking process.
- Can be used for melting (e.g. butter, chocolate), making sauces, poaching fish, defrosting or heating up foods.
- Glass, most plastics and ceramics (china) can be used as dishes – **not metal**.

Check your understanding

Tested

1 Identify two methods of cooking vegetables that retain more vitamin C than boiling. **(2 marks)**

2 Identify two cooking methods that tenderise meat. **(2 marks)**

3 Give three advantages of cooking in a microwave. **(3 marks)**

10.1 Basic ingredients – properties and functions

Fats and oils ━━━━━━━━━━━━━━━━━━━━━━━━━━ Revised

Fats are solid and oils are liquid.

Exam tip

The topic of basic ingredients forms a basis for your understanding of 'The effects of cooking'. It is recommended that these areas are revised together. Make sure you know the function of each ingredient in a range of different recipes and foods.

Function of fat	Reason for use	Examples
Spreads	Add **flavour** and **lubricate** food	Butter, margarine, cream cheese
Shortening	Fat stops **gluten** making long strands (fat **shortens** them) Baked mixture has a 'melt-in-mouth' texture	Pastries, shortbread, cakes
Frosting and creams	Add **flavour** and **texture**	Buttercream icing, chocolate frosting
Flavouring and moisture	Fat stops water evaporating giving a longer shelf-life	Focaccia bread, fruit cake, biscuits
Trap air to make mixture rise	Margarine and butter **trap air bubbles** when beaten together with sugar	Cake mixtures

Function of oil	Reason for use	Examples
Shallow, deep and stir-frying	Adds flavour and crisps foods	Shallow: eggs, pancakes Deep: battered fish, falafel Stir-fry: vegetables, meat
Sautéing	Brings out the flavour of food	Onions (the natural sugar in them caramelises), root vegetables
Roasting	Water evaporates, oil adds flavour, natural flavours intensify	Meat, poultry, vegetables
Salad dressings, sauces	Adds texture and flavour	Mayonnaise, vinaigrette, hollandaise sauce
Dips for bread	Alternative to butter or margarine	Oils flavoured with herbs

Function of eggs	Explanation of use	Examples
Trap air	**Protein stretches** when whisked or beaten Air trapped as tiny bubbles (**aeration**)	Whisked sponges, meringue, soufflés
Bind ingredients	Protein **coagulates** when heated Binds other ingredients together	Potato croquettes, fish cakes
Coat and protect	Fried foods dipped in egg and breadcrumbs or batter (contains egg) Protein **coagulates** and forms protective seal around food	Fish, apple fritters
Thicken foods	Protein coagulates and thickens foods	Sauces, e.g. egg custard
Prevent oil and water separating (emulsifying)	Lecithin in egg yolk holds oil and water together (**emulsification**) Lecithin (**emulsifier**)	Mayonnaise
Glazing	Protein forms golden brown colour with starch and sugar in baked products	Scones, pies, mashed potatoes, e.g. fish pie
Enriching	Eggs contain a wide range of nutrients	Sauces, pastry, pasta, stuffings
Garnishing	Hard boiled eggs – sliced, quartered	Salads

Function of sugar (sucrose)	Reason for use	Examples
Flavouring	Humans have a preference for sweet foods Sugar is added to many types of foods Brown sugar adds extra flavour from **molasses** in it	Confectionery, biscuits, cakes, yeast products, breakfast cereals, soft drinks
Texture	Sugar crystals add texture depending on size	Icing sugar (very fine), demerera (crunchy)
	Boiled sugar makes sweets	Toffees, fudge, boiled sweets, caramels
	Sugar softens gluten in baked mixtures (e.g. cakes) to make them have a tender 'crumb'; too much makes mixtures collapse	Cakes, biscuits, sponge puddings
Trap air	Whisked sugar and egg or beaten sugar and margarine or butter trap air to make a cake rise	Sponges, cakes
Add colour	Caramelises (goes brown) when heated	Cakes, crème caramel, toffee, buns

Wheat flour contains **gluten** (protein).

- Gluten absorbs water and forms long, stretchy strands.
- Gluten allows doughs and mixtures to rise when gas bubbles are made, e.g. by yeast or baking powder.
- Coagulates when heated – dough/mixture sets.
- Wheat flour contains **starch** (carbohydrate).
- Starch is found in **granules**.
- When mixed with water and heated, starch granules **absorb** the water and **soften** and **swell**.

- The mixture **thickens**.
- Some starch granules break and release the starch, which forms a gel; this is **gelatinisation**.
- Starch is converted to **dextrin** when dry heated (e.g. toasted).

Wheat flour	Protein content	Reason for use	Examples
Strong plain flour	More than 10%	Makes lots of gluten strands so makes stretchy dough that rises well	Breads, buns, choux pastry, puff pastry, batters (Yorkshire puddings)
Soft plain flour	Less than 10%	Makes less stretchy, more tender dough Can be easily 'shortened' by fat	Short crust pastry, cakes, biscuits
Self raising flour	Less than 10%	Makes less stretchy, more tender dough that rises when baked due to the addition of **baking powder** Can be easily 'shortened' by fat	Cakes, biscuits, scones
Durum wheat flour	More than 10%	Gluten is very tough so does not stretch well	Fresh pasta dough

↑ **Figure 10.1 Making dough**

Check your understanding

Tested

1 Identify three functions of fat. *(3 marks)*
2 Give three functions of egg. *(3 marks)*
3 Give an example of eggs being used to thicken a product. *(1 mark)*
4 Name two functions of sugar in a Victoria sandwich. *(2 marks)*
5 Give one reason for sieving flour when making cakes. *(1 mark)*
6 Name two herbs or spices you could use in a curry. *(2 marks)*

10.2 The use of raising agents in cooking

Key facts

● Many baked items have a light texture.

● Baked mixtures have to be **raised** during baking.

● **Raising agents** are used to put **gases** into baked mixtures.

● Gases **expand** when heated and raise mixtures. When the mixture sets, the bubbles give texture.

● Also known as **leavening agents** – leavening means 'to lift up'.

● Gases used are **air** (a mixture of gases), **carbon dioxide** (CO_2), **steam** (water as a gas).

Chemical raising agents

Baking powder

● A mixture of **an alkali and an acid**:

  ● bicarbonate of soda and cream of tartar create carbon dioxide bubbles

  ● an alkali and an acid and moisture and heat create CO_2.

● If bicarbonate of soda is used on its own it leaves a soapy, bitter taste – it is only used like this in strong-flavoured mixtures, e.g. gingerbread.

● Used for scones, cakes, biscuits.

Yeast

● Yeast is a tiny, single-celled plant; microscopic.

● Yeast produces carbon dioxide gas if given the right conditions, i.e.:

  ● yeast and sugar/starch, and moisture, warmth and time create CO_2 gas and alcohol (the alcohol evaporates in the oven).

● The whole process is called **fermentation**.

● Used for breads, buns, doughnuts, beer and wine making.

● Yeast is available:

  ● fresh and dried (both need to be activated with warm water and sugar)

  ● or fast acting dried (added directly to flour).

> **Exam tip**
>
> A higher order skill is to describe how something, such as bread, rises. This may seem daunting but attempt it. By correctly mentioning yeast and the steam created by hot air you will gain marks.

Mechanical raising agents

Air

● Air is a mixture of gases.

● Air is put into mixtures by:

- **sieving flour** (air trapped between flour particles)
- **creaming** (beating with wooden spoon or whisk) **fat** (butter or margarine) and **sugar** together (air is trapped and held in place by egg, which sets around the bubbles when the mixture is baked)
- **whisking whole eggs or egg whites with sugar**, which traps a lot of air in the egg protein
- **folding and rolling** pastry layers in puff or flaky pastry, which traps air. When baked, the air expands, the fat in the pastry melts and steam from the water also makes the pastry rise
- **rubbing fat into flour** – traps some air.

● Air is used for cakes, biscuits, pastries, mousses, soufflés, sponge puddings, sponge flans, swiss rolls.

Steam

● Steam is water vapour.

● It is used for mixtures that contain a lot of water, e.g. batters, choux pastry, puff pastry.

● The oven must be hot to make steam quickly.

● Do not open the oven door while baking or the mixture will collapse.

↑ Figure 10.2

> ### Exam tip
>
> Be prepared to look at a recipe or method and name the raising agent or method that causes the food to rise. For example, for a Victoria sandwich:
>
> ● The ingredients include self-raising flour (which contains baking powder).
>
> ● Sieving the flour introduces air.
>
> ● Creaming the fat and sugar also traps air.

↑ Figure 10.3

Check your understanding

1 State two ways air can be added to a mixture. *(2 marks)*

2 Describe how bread rises. *(5 marks)*

3 Name two chemical raising agents. *(2 marks)*

11.1 Cooking breads, pastries, cakes, biscuits and scones

Key facts ──────────────────────────────── Revised ☐

- **Basic ingredients**: flour, fat, sugar, eggs, other liquids (milk, fruit juice, water), raising agents, flavourings, other ingredients (nuts, seeds, dried fruit, fresh fruit, vegetables).

- Ingredients react in different ways when heated.

> **Exam tip**
>
> The questions on this topic are likely to focus on the changes that take place when a food item is cooked. Do not panic, no matter which recipes you are presented with, as the principles are similar. For example, flour is a starch, which sets the mixture. Any fat melts and is absorbed by the starch.

Changes that take place when breads and buns are baked

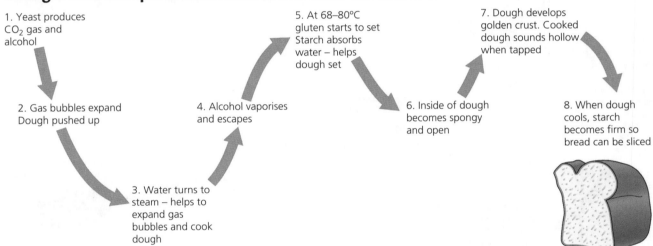

1. Yeast produces CO_2 gas and alcohol

2. Gas bubbles expand Dough pushed up

3. Water turns to steam – helps to expand gas bubbles and cook dough

4. Alcohol vaporises and escapes

5. At 68–80°C gluten starts to set Starch absorbs water – helps dough set

6. Inside of dough becomes spongy and open

7. Dough develops golden crust. Cooked dough sounds hollow when tapped

8. When dough cools, starch becomes firm so bread can be sliced

↑ **Figure 11.1**

Buns cook in the same way, but:

- they contain egg, which helps the dough set
- the sugar they contain melts and softens the gluten
- added fat melts and is absorbed by the starch.

Changes that take place when pastries are baked

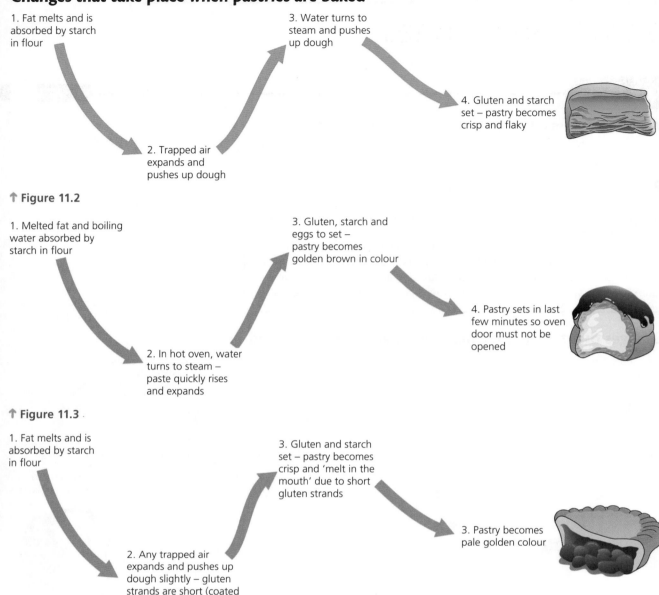

1. Fat melts and is absorbed by starch in flour

2. Trapped air expands and pushes up dough

3. Water turns to steam and pushes up dough

4. Gluten and starch set – pastry becomes crisp and flaky

↑ **Figure 11.2**

1. Melted fat and boiling water absorbed by starch in flour

2. In hot oven, water turns to steam – paste quickly rises and expands

3. Gluten, starch and eggs to set – pastry becomes golden brown in colour

4. Pastry sets in last few minutes so oven door must not be opened

↑ **Figure 11.3**

1. Fat melts and is absorbed by starch in flour

2. Any trapped air expands and pushes up dough slightly – gluten strands are short (coated with fat) so dough does not stretch much

3. Gluten and starch set – pastry becomes crisp and 'melt in the mouth' due to short gluten strands

3. Pastry becomes pale golden colour

↑ **Figure 11.4**

Enriched shortcrust pastry cooks in the same way, but:

● added sugar gives a golden colour (the sugar caramelises)

● added egg helps the pastry set.

Changes that take place when cakes are baked

There are three methods of making a cake; each method has some differences. The table on the next page shows how all cakes go through some of the same processes – for example, eggs help the mixture to set at stage 2.

	Melting method	Creaming method (all-in-one)	Whisking method
Stage 1	Baking powder or bicarbonate of soda give off CO_2 gas – this expands and makes the mixture rise	Trapped air bubbles expand and push up mixture	
Stage 2	Eggs help the mixture set and add colour		
Stage 3	Sugar melts and turns to syrup – this softens the gluten and makes the cake tender		
Stage 4	Fat melts and is absorbed by the starch in the flour		n/a
Stage 5	n/a	Fat shortens the gluten strands and makes the cake tender	n/a
Stage 6	n/a	Baking powder gives off CO_2 gas – this expands in heat and makes the cake rise	n/a
Stage 7	Starch and gluten set and form a fine network of bubbles – gives the cake a spongy texture		
Stage 8	Sugar caramelises and adds colour		
Stage 9	A golden crust is formed on the outside		

↑ **Figure 11.5 Cake made by the melting method**

↑ **Figure 11.6 Cake made all-in-one**

↑ **Figure 11.7 Cake made by the whisking method**

Changes that take place when biscuits are baked

Shortbread biscuits change like shortcrust pastry (see previous page).

Cookies:

1. Fat melts and is absorbed by starch in flour

2. Any trapped air expands and pushes up dough slightly

3. Baking powder/bicarbonate of soda gives off CO_2 gas – expands and makes mixture rise

4. Starch and gluten set – cookies become crisp and 'melt in the mouth' due to short gluten strands

5. The heat makes cookies have a pale golden colour (unless they contain cocoa)

6. Chocolate chips melt and add moisture

↑ **Figure 11.8**

Changes that take place when scones are baked

1. Fat melts and is absorbed by starch in flour

2. Water (in milk) turns to steam – makes dough rise quickly and expand

3. Baking powder/bicarbonate of soda gives off CO_2 gas – expands in heat – makes scones rise

4. Starch and gluten set – form a fine network of bubbles – gives light, spongy texture

5. If sugar added – caramelises and gives colour and flavour

6. If cheese added – melts and adds moisture and flavour

7. Golden crust forms on outside

↑ **Figure 11.9**

Check your understanding — Tested

1. Explain how puff pastry rises. *(6 marks)*

2. Give two characteristics of well-cooked choux pastry. *(2 marks)*

3. Describe three changes that occur when a cupcake is baked in the oven. *(6 marks)*

4. State one function of flour (starch) when shortbread is baked in the oven. *(1 mark)*

5. When scones are cooked, water from the milk turns to steam, which makes the scones rise. True or false? *(1 mark)*

11.2 Cooking sauces and batters

Sauces

Sauces are added to foods to:

- add moisture, flavour, colour, nutrients (enrich)
- bind ingredients together
- make meals varied.

> **Exam tip**
>
> This is often a poorly answered topic; when describing gelatinisation it is too vague to state 'liquid binds to flour'. Do not confuse gelatinisation with coagulation.

Sauce name	Main ingredients	What happens when cooked or prepared
Béchamel or roux	Milk, flour, fat (butter)	• starch granules soften, absorb fat and milk, swell • sauce thickens • some starch escapes granules and forms a gel (gelatinises)
Mayonnaise (no heat used)	Egg yolk, salt, pepper, vinegar or lemon juice, oil	• lecithin (egg yolk), vinegar, salt and pepper prevent oil from separating out • mayonnaise gradually thickens
Coulis (fruit sauce)	Soft fruit (e.g. berries), sugar, water, cooked vegetable purée	• puréed fruit or vegetable gives texture • thins out with water or lemon juice
Tomato sauce	Tomatoes, onions, celery, roasted red peppers, fresh herbs, seasoning, butter, flour, stock	• starch granules absorb fat and stock, swell • sauce thickens • some starch escapes granules and forms a gel (gelatinises) • vegetables add texture • can be puréed
Pesto (no heat used)	Fresh herbs (e.g. basil, coriander), garlic, pine nuts, grated parmesan cheese, olive oil	• puréed herbs, pine nuts, cheese, garlic give texture • oil adds smoothness
Cornflour	Milk, cornflour, sugar, vanilla	• starch granules absorb milk, swell • sauce thickens • some starch escapes granules and forms a gel (gelatinises)
Egg custard sauce (sauce Anglais)	Eggs, milk, sugar, vanilla	• egg protein gradually coagulates • sauce thickens • must be heated gently to prevent protein cooking too fast

Batters

- The main ingredients of a batter are eggs, flour and liquid (usually milk).
- Batters are made into pancakes, crêpes, Yorkshire puddings, 'toad-in-the-hole', fritters (coated and fried foods), tempura (Japanese batter), and coatings for deep fried foods, e.g. fish.
- When a batter is fried:
  - the egg and wheat protein set
  - the starch absorbs the liquid and some cooking oil
  - the outside becomes crispy.
- When a batter is baked:
  - the liquid turns to steam and the mixture rises
  - the egg and wheat protein set
  - the starch absorbs the liquid and some cooking oil
  - the outside becomes crispy.

↑ Figure 11.10 Pancakes: an example of a batter

Check your understanding — Tested

1 Give three reasons for adding a sauce to a food. *(3 marks)*

2 Starch can be used to thicken a sauce. Describe how starch thickens
   a sauce. *(5 marks)*

3 State the three main ingredients in a batter. *(3 marks)*

4 State what happens to the following ingredients in a baked batter: *(3 marks)*

   a) the liquid

   b) the protein

   c) the starch.

11.3 Cooking meat, poultry and fish

Key facts

- Meat and poultry are cooked:
  - to make them safe to eat (to destroy harmful bacteria)
  - to develop flavour
  - to make them easy to chew, swallow and digest.
- Meat and poultry are made of bundles of **muscle fibres**:
  - muscle fibres contain proteins (**actin** and **myosin**)
  - big muscle fibres are tougher than small ones
  - muscle fibres are bound together with **connective tissue**
  - connective tissue is made of proteins (**collagen** and **elastin**), these make meat tough
  - **fat** also found between the muscle fibres and under the skin.

> **Exam tip**
>
> The reasons for cooking food and the changes that take place are common short answer questions.

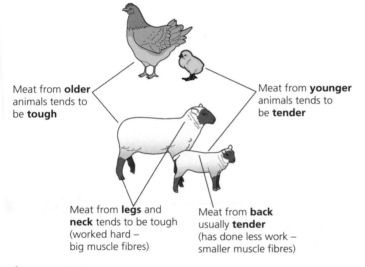

Meat from **older** animals tends to be **tough**

Meat from **younger** animals tends to be **tender**

Meat from **legs** and **neck** tends to be tough (worked hard – big muscle fibres)

Meat from **back** usually **tender** (has done less work – smaller muscle fibres)

↑ **Figure 11.11**

To tenderise meat **before** cooking:

- **score** (cut) muscle fibres to shorten them
- **pound** (hit with a meat hammer) muscles to break them up
- **marinate** (soak) in acid (e.g. lemon juice or vinegar) or alcohol (e.g. red wine) to change the protein structure.

When meat is cooked

	Changes that happen when meat is cooked
Texture	• actin and myosin **denature** (change) • meat becomes **firmer** and **shrinks** • tough cuts (e.g. leg, neck) will become tender if cooked slowly in liquid (e.g. stew) because **collagen** changes to **gelatine**
Flavour	• **fat** between muscle fibres melts and adds flavour and moisture • **fat** under the skin melts and the skin becomes crispy • when actin and myosin denature, flavoured liquid inside the muscle fibres is squeezed out; this liquid is called **extractives** (more is found in large muscle fibres) • extractives come to the meat surface when it is grilled, roasted or fried • extractives are used to make **gravy**
Colour	• colour is caused by protein **myoglobin** and some **haemoglobin** (from blood) • meat is usually **darker** in parts of the animal or bird that do the most physical activity • red meat changes to **brown** colour (and pink meat changes to white) during cooking
Nutritional value	• overcooked meat is dry and less digestible • **B vitamins** (especially B_1 thiamin) are damaged by heat • some minerals are squeezed out of muscle fibres • **fat** can be trimmed to reduce energy value • **grilling** lets fat run out, which reduces energy value

Fish

● Has **less connective tissue** than meat. It is more tender and cooks more quickly.

● White fish is **low in fat**. It must be cooked gently so it doesn't go dry.

● When it is cooked, the flesh from fish should come away from the bones easily.

● Oily fish has **fat in muscle** and is less likely to go dry.

Check your understanding ————————————————————————— Tested

1 Describe two changes that take place when meat is cooked. *(4 marks)*

2 Describe how when roasting a chicken you could check to see if the chicken is fully cooked. *(2 marks)*

11.4 Cooking vegetables and fruit

Key facts

- Many fruits and vegetables can be eaten raw.
- Need to be cooked carefully to preserve **flavour, colour, texture and nutrients**.
- Methods of cooking are boiling, simmering, steaming, stewing, stir-frying, frying, roasting, baking, microwaving.

Exam tip
When a question asks you to describe something, answer it by making a point and then expanding on that point. For example, when describing how to cook vegetables to minimise the loss of vitamin C, steaming is a better cooking method as the vegetables are not placed directly in the water. This means there is less chance of the vitamin C leaching into the water; it is also a quicker method of cooking.

Changes that happen when vegetables and fruits are cooked	
Texture	• cooking **softens** the plant cell walls, this releases water, softens texture • vegetables lose **bulk** • cells **separate** and vegetables break up and go mushy • **starch** granules absorb water, soften and swell; this makes vegetables tender and drier
Flavour	• flavour is **intensified** (becomes **concentrated**) when cooked, e.g. carrots become sweeter • natural chemicals are released to add to the flavour, e.g. natural sugars in onion **caramelise** • when roasting, **water** is driven out so flavour is **intensified**
Colour	**green** vegetables: • become bright green, then change to olive green, then become a grey/green colour (which is not appetising) • **cook** in the minimum water for the shortest time; **serve** straightaway to **preserve** flavour, colour, texture and nutrients
	red and purple vegetables are changed by acids (which makes them bright red) or alkalis (which makes them blue)
	yellow and orange vegetables are stable when cooked
Nutritional value	• cutting and bruising damages cells, releases enzymes, destroys nutrients (e.g. vitamin C) and antioxidants • exposure to light and oxygen destroys nutrients (e.g. vitamin C) and antioxidants; chop just before cooking to prevent this • vitamin C and other water soluble vitamins leach into cooking water – use the minimum amount of water and use the left-over water in gravies or soups to save nutrients • heat destroys vitamin C and other nutrients – cook for the shortest time possible and serve straightaway • some starch is released, which makes it easier to digest • some beta carotene is released, which enables our body to use it

Check your understanding

1 State three ways vegetables can be cooked. *(3 marks)*
2 Describe two changes that occur when a carrot is boiled. *(4 marks)*
3 Identify two ways to prepare vegetables to minimise the loss of vitamin C. *(2 marks)*

11.5 The effects of acids and alkalis on foods

Key facts
Revised

Acids

- Have a sour taste that makes foods sharp and zesty.
- Are found naturally in some foods.
- Add flavour to foods.
- Help preserve foods (many micro-organisms cannot live in acidic conditions).
- Act as antioxidants, e.g. vitamin C.
- Help jam to set.
- Change the texture of foods by denaturing protein, e.g. in cheese making and marinating meat.
- Prevent fruits going brown when cut, e.g. adding lemon juice to apples, bananas.
- Examples:
  - citric acid – found in citrus fruits, e.g. lemons, oranges
  - malic acid – found in apples
  - tartaric acid – found in grapes
  - ethanoic acid (old name acetic acid) – found in vinegar
  - phosphoric acid – added to fizzy drinks, e.g. cola
  - ascorbic acid (vitamin C) – found in many fruits and vegetables.

Alkalis

- Few found naturally in foods.
- **Bicarbonate of soda** is a weak alkali used as a raising agent.

> **Exam tip**
>
> Short questions on this topic often relate to the function of acids in food, especially for preservation.

Check your understanding
Tested

1 You have cut an apple and left it on the side. Name one ingredient that could be added to the apple to stop it going brown. *(1 mark)*

2 Give two reasons why acids are used in food products. *(1 mark)*

3 Name one alkali used in cooking. *(1 mark)*

12 The function of additives in food products

Key facts

- Food additives are substances put into processed food products by manufacturers.
- There are three groups of additives:
  - **natural** substances from foods
  - additives that are like natural ones but have been copied and made in a **laboratory**
  - **synthetic (man-made)** additives made in a laboratory (these are not found in natural foods).

Type of additive	Reason this type is used in food products
Preservatives	• to increase the shelf life • to prevent the growth of micro-organisms • to prevent or slow down natural spoilage of the food
Colourings	• to improve the natural colour of a processed food • to change the colour of a food
Flavourings and sweeteners	• to enhance (improve) the natural flavour of a processed food • to make more varieties of a product, such as potato crisps • to create new products with unusual flavours, such as sweets and drinks
Emulsifiers and stabilisers	• to make sure the product stays stable by preventing ingredients from separating out when it is stored • to make the product easier for a manufacturer to produce • to give the same texture, shape and consistency each time the product is made, so that customers know what to expect
Thickeners	To improve the texture and 'mouth feel' of products such as yogurts and custards

- Additives have to be **approved as safe** for use by the government and the European Union (EU).
- Additives approved for use in foods by the EU are given an **E number**; they have to be regularly tested for safety.
- Additives must be **listed on a food label** so consumers know what is in the foods they buy – this helps people to understand what is in their food.
- Some people are concerned about the **amount** and **mixture** of additives found in different foods, especially for the short- and long-term health of people (particularly children).
- Some additives may be linked to certain **health** and **behaviour problems** (e.g. cancer, hyperactive behaviour).

Exam tip

Reasons for the use of additives is the main focus, so ensure you know the five main reasons:
- Preservation
- Colouring
- Flavouring/sweetening
- Emulsifier/stabiliser
- Thickener

Check your understanding

1 Give two reasons why additives are used in food products. *(2 marks)*
2 Name one additive added to white flour by law. *(1 mark)*

13.1 Food spoilage

Key facts

Revised

Changes in the food make it unfit to eat

Food has 'off' flavours and 'off' smell

Spoilage occurs by natural decay or contamination by micro-organisms

Food has changed colour / texture

↑ **Figure 13.1**

- **Perishable foods** contain a lot of water and nutrients. They spoil quickly.

- Processed and preserved perishable foods will spoil once opened, thawed, mixed with water.

- Food labelling for perishable foods:

  - **'use by' date** – food must be eaten by this date for safety

  - **storage instructions** – e.g. fridge and freezer temperatures and times

  - **cooking instructions** – i.e. oven temperatures and times; microwave power setting and times

  - **'display until' date** – sometimes used by shops to make sure food is sold before its use by date expires.

- Food labelling for non-perishable foods uses **'best before'** or **'best before end'** (month/year) – food is best before these dates, but will start to change texture or flavour after this so will not be nice to eat.

- Always use stocks of food in **rotation** (use oldest first).

- **Natural decay** of food is caused by:

  - moisture loss

  - action of **enzymes**

  - contamination by micro-organisms.

↑ **Figure 13.2 Some perishable foods**

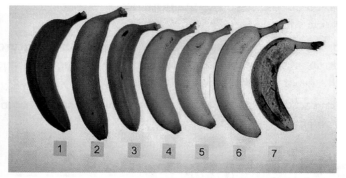

↑ **Figure 13.3 The natural changes in a banana over time**

Micro-organisms

● very small

● **bacteria, moulds, yeasts** (there are many types in each group)

● produce **waste products** or **toxins** (poisons) or make food inedible by being there

● **pathogenic (harmful)** micro-organisms may cause **food poisoning**

● non-harmful micro-organisms are used in the making of cheese, beer, wine, yeast extract and yogurt.

Bacteria

● bacteria are tiny and therefore are found in many places: soil, water, dust, animals, humans, plants, sewage, food, fabrics

● there are many types, and many shapes

● bacteria need the following **conditions** to grow and multiply: **suitable temperature** (usually 37°C), **moisture, food**

● bacteria **reproduce** (multiply) by dividing in two every 20 minutes (in ideal conditions)

● one bacteria becomes millions in a few hours.

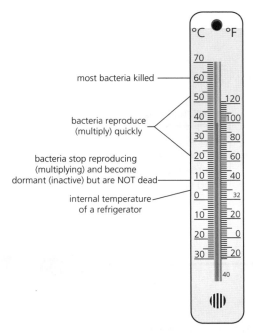

↑ **Figure 13.4**

To prevent spoilage by bacteria:

● cool leftover hot foods to 0–5°C within 1½ hours

● use leftover foods within 24 hours and heat to at least 70°C

● **high concentrations** of salt, sugar or acid destroy bacteria.

Moulds

● moulds are tiny plants (fungi)

● moulds need the following **conditions** to grow and multiply: **suitable temperature** (usually 37°C), **moisture, food**

● can grow slowly in cold temperatures

- **harmless** moulds are used to make some cheeses, e.g. Stilton, Danish blue, Camembert
- a special mould called a **mycoprotein** is used to make the high protein food 'Quorn®'.

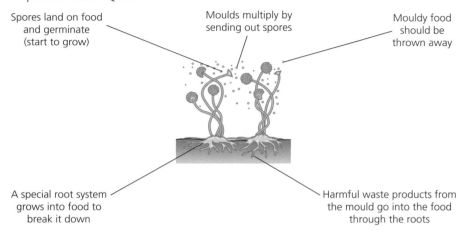

Spores land on food and germinate (start to grow)

Moulds multiply by sending out spores

Mouldy food should be thrown away

A special root system grows into food to break it down

Harmful waste products from the mould go into the food through the roots

⬆ **Figure 13.5**

Yeasts

- yeasts are tiny single-celled fungi
- found in air, soil, surface of fruits
- can grow without oxygen
- reproduce by sending out a 'bud', which breaks off to form another yeast cell
- yeasts need the following **conditions** to grow and multiply: **suitable temperature** (usually 37°C), **moisture, food**
- **dormant** (inactive) in cold conditions
- killed at 100°C
- spoil jams, fruit yogurts and fruits by **fermenting** the sugars to CO_2 gas and alcohol.

> **Exam tip**
>
> This is an important topic. Make sure you know the three types of micro-organism and the signs of food spoilage.

Check your understanding ─────────────────────────────── Tested ▢

1 State two perishable foods. *(2 marks)*

2 Match the following dates and descriptions: *(3 marks)*

Best before date	The date by which the food should be eaten to ensure it is safe.
Display until date	The food will be at its best condition before this date (relates to flavour/texture).
Use by date	The food must be sold by this date (but is still safe to eat).

13.2 Food preservation at home

Key facts

Preservation is the treatment of food to prevent or slow down food spoilage by decay or micro-organisms.

Method of preserving food	How it works
Using high temperatures	• kills many micro-organisms • stops the action of enzymes
Using low temperatures	• makes micro-organisms inactive so they cannot grow or reproduce • slows down chemical reactions
Drying food (dehydration)	• kills many micro-organisms by removing water from them • prevents some chemical reactions from taking place inside food
Using acids	• kills many micro-organisms • stops the action of enzymes
Using sugar or salt	Kills many micro-organisms by removing water from them
Controlling the atmosphere inside packaging and removing oxygen	• stops micro-organisms from growing • stops other micro-organisms from getting into the food

Jam-making

● Uses **high temperatures** and **sugar** to destroy micro-organisms (mainly yeast).

● **Heat** and **sugar** and **pectin** (from fruit) makes jam form a **gel** when cooled.

● Boiling jam must go into **hot, sterilised jars** and be **sealed** to prevent other micro-organisms from contaminating it.

Pickling

● Uses vinegar **(ethanoic/acetic acid)** to preserve vegetables, fruits, fish (herrings), hard boiled eggs.

● Food is packed into jars, filled with vinegar and then sealed and left to mature for a few weeks.

● **Pickles, relishes and chutneys** are thick, sweet sauces made from fruits or vegetables, sugar, salt, vinegar.

↑ **Figure 13.6**

Drying

● Herbs and some fruits can be dried.

● **Herbs** are tied in bundles and left in warm, circulating air.

● **Water** is removed and the flavour intensifies (becomes concentrated); store in air tight jars.

● **Fruits**, e.g. apple slices – dried by placing on trays in the oven at a low temperature for a few hours to remove water.

Freezing

● Many foods can be frozen.

● Temperature must not be higher than −18°C to **store** frozen foods.

● Temperature must not be higher than −21°C to −24°C to **fast freeze** fresh foods.

- **Fast freezing** is when foods are frozen quickly to **prevent large ice crystals** forming inside them.
- Large ice crystals will damage food texture and make it mushy when thawed.
- Vegetables should be **blanched** (dipped into boiling water for a few seconds then into iced water) to stop **enzyme action**.
- Freezing slows chemical reactions in foods but does not stop them – the flavour, texture, colour of the food gradually changes while frozen.
- Treat **defrosted food** like fresh food, as the **dormant micro-organisms** will start to reproduce again.
- Food should be defrosted thoroughly, especially chicken. Bacteria can remain alive in the cold parts of unthawed food when it is cooking.
- Defrost food in a cool place (e.g. a refrigerator); this prevents the outside temperature of the food becoming too warm.

Bottling

- Fruits and vegetables can be preserved in jars in either **brine** (salt and water) or **syrup** (made from sugar and water).
- The clean, sterilised jars are sealed then heated to **sterilise** (destroy harmful micro-organisms) the food.
- Jars are cooled and can be kept preserved for several months **if not opened**.

Salting

- One of the oldest forms of preservation.
- Micro-organisms cannot grow in high salt concentrations.
- Preserves foods such as cheese, sausages (e.g. dried chorizo, salami), fish (e.g. Jamaican and Chinese salt fish, kippered herrings), meat (e.g. beef jerky, ham, bacon, corned beef).
- Adds flavour.

↑ Figure 13.7

> **Exam tip**
>
> In the exam do not confuse commercial preservation with home preservation – always read the question.

> **Check your understanding**   Tested
>
> 1 Explain how drying preserves food.   *(2 marks)*
> 2 Identify three foods that can be preserved by pickling.   *(3 marks)*

13.3 Commercial food preservation

Key facts

Revised ☐

- Most foods from a supermarket are processed in some way.
- Many methods of preservation are used commercially.

> **Exam tip**
>
> The course is designed to be more applicable to home situations, therefore you do not need to know the commercial preservation methods in great detail. Know the names of the different types, e.g. modified atmosphere packaging (MAP), and how it works, i.e. MAP works by changing the atmosphere around the food in the packaging, slowing the micro-organism growth.

Processes using this principle	Examples of foods preserved this way	Other notes
Using high temperatures		
Pasteurisation	Milk, fruit juice, ice cream, dried eggs, wines, fresh soups	• food is heated to a high temperature for a short time to kill **pathogenic** (harmful) and some **spoilage** micro-organisms • little effect on nutrients and flavour
Sterilisation	Milk, low acid canned foods	• very high temperatures used • **all micro-organisms are killed** • affects flavour, colour and nutrients
Ultra heat treatment (UHT) – sometimes called 'long-life'	Milk, soup, cream, condensed milk, fruit juices, sauces	• food is heated to a high temperature for very short time • little effect on flavour, colour or nutrients • packaged in special air tight, layered cartons • can be kept **unopened** at room temperature for many months
Canning	Vegetables, fruits, meat, fish, soups, milk products, baby food, drinks	• uses **hermetically sealed** (air tight) metal cans • heated to sterilise contents after sealing • other hermetically sealed cartons are also used, e.g. plastic pouches, cartons, plastic trays
Using low temperatures		
Cook-chilling	Ready-made foods and meals, sauces	• cooked foods are quickly **cooled** and stored at low temperatures to be heated up at home within a few days • **growth of micro-organisms is slowed** by cool temperatures
Fluidised bed freezing	Peas, sweetcorn, berries	Food does not stick together when frozen
Plate freezing	Fish, 'boil-in-the-bag' foods, ready meals	Food is put into contact with metal freezing plates
Air-blast freezing	Fish, chicken, pizzas, desserts	Cold air (between −30ºC and −40ºC) circulated around the food
Cryogenic freezing	Expensive foods, e.g. prawns, strawberries	Food is frozen with liquid nitrogen (−196ºC)
Using dehydration		
1. Roller, spray and tunnel drying (hot air used to remove moisture) **2. Accelerated freeze drying** (moisture removed by sublimation)	Milk, coffee, fruits, vegetables	• dried foods: are light, take up less space, are cheaper and easier to transport and store, have a long shelf-life • flavour, texture, colour and nutrients affected (especially vitamin C) • treat as fresh foods once water has been added • **sublimation** means that ice is changed instantly to water vapour; foods dried in this way will mix well with water

(Continued)

(Continued)

Processes using this principle	Examples of foods preserved this way	Other notes
Using chemicals (chemical preservatives) – some examples		
Salt	Fish, meat, cheese, vegetables	• water is drawn out of micro-organisms • salt is added directly or dissolved in water (**brine**)
Sugar	Jams, glacé cherries, condensed milk, cakes	Works in a similar way to salt, but higher concentrations are needed
Sodium benzoate	Fruit juice, pickles, salad dressings	Stops mould and yeasts growing
Sulphur dioxide	Wine, beers, fruit juice, sausages	• stops some bacteria and moulds growing • stops browning caused by enzymes
Sorbic acid	Hard cheese, bread, jam, syrup	Stops mould and yeasts and some bacteria growing
Using fermentation		
Natural process	Vinegar, olives, salami, yogurt, beer, soy sauce, blue cheese	Specially produced micro-organisms turn carbohydrate into an acid to preserve the food
Using physical means		
Modified atmosphere packaging (MAP)	Meat products, fish products	• the atmosphere around the food is changed inside the packaging so growth of micro-organisms is slowed • usually chilled
Vacuum packaging	Meat products, fish products, cooked vegetables, fresh pasta	• oxygen is removed • stops growth of some micro-organisms • must be chilled to prevent growth of pathogenic micro-organisms
Smoking	Meat, fish, cheese, some vegetables	• food is held over smoke • chemicals in wood preserve and add flavour • food is usually dipped in acid or salt solution first
Irradiation	Potatoes, cereals, vegetables	• gamma rays fired into food • stops potatoes sprouting; kills insects and parasites

Check your understanding

Tested

1 Name two commercial preservation methods suitable for vegetables. *(2 marks)*

2 Explain how salt preserves a food. *(2 marks)*

14.1 Causes and effects of food poisoning

Key facts ────────────────────────────────────── Revised ☐

Food poisoning (FP) is an **acute** illness caused by eating **contaminated food**.

Symptoms of FP (can take a few hours or days to appear):

● nausea and vomiting

● severe abdominal (stomach and intestinal) pain

● diarrhoea (may contain blood)

● high or low body temperature

● headache and/or body ache

● weakness and lack of energy

● very rarely, death.

FP is caused by

● bacteria, viruses, toxins from moulds

● toxins and waste products from micro-organisms

● irritation of the lining of the gastro-intestinal tract (stomach, intestines)

● some types of bacteria that enter the bloodstream and other organs of the body and cause damage.

FP can last for several days or weeks.

Vulnerable groups who are more likely to get FP

● Babies and young children (their immune systems are not fully developed to fight infection).

● Pregnant women (FP can damage the unborn baby).

● The elderly (their immune systems are weaker).

● People with weak immune systems (e.g. due to HIV/AIDS, leukaemia).

FP should be reported to the **Environmental Health Department** of your local authority to investigate the cause.

● Many people do not report that they have had FP.

Why do people get FP?

● More food eaten outside the home.

● Food may not have been prepared hygienically.

● Lack of knowledge and understanding about storing, preparing and cooking foods.

● Intensive farming; disease spreads easily when animals, birds, fish are kept together in large numbers.

> **Exam tip**
> This topic is often linked to prevention of food poisoning and food hygiene rules.

↑ **Figure 14.1**

Common bacteria that cause food poisoning

Food poisoning bacteria	Examples of foods where it is found	Symptoms of food poisoning	How it gets into food
Salmonella (all types)	Raw eggs, chicken, meat, cheese, mayonnaise, salad dressing, bean sprouts	Severe abdominal pain Diarrhoea Nausea Vomiting High body temperature	Contamination from raw foods Dirty water Pests People
Staphylococcus aureus	Cooked meat, poultry, eggs, cream, salad, milk, some dried foods	Severe abdominal pain Diarrhoea Nausea Vomiting Low body temperature Collapse	Human nose, mouth, skin Cuts and skin infections Raw (untreated) milk from infected cows or goats
Bacillus cereus	Cooked rice, herbs, dairy products, meat, starchy food, soups, vegetables	Severe abdominal pain Watery diarrhoea Nausea Vomiting	Dust, soil
Escherichia coli (E.coli)	Cooked food, water, milk, seafood, salad, meat	Severe abdominal pain Diarrhoea Nausea Vomiting Fever	Human sewage Dirty water Raw meat
Clostridium perfringens	Meat, poultry, gravy, stews	Severe abdominal pain Diarrhoea	Sewage Dust, soil Animals Insects Raw meat
Listeria monocytogenes	Coleslaw, soft unpasteurised cheese, cook-chill ready meals, pâté	Fever Diarrhoea Flu-like illness Blood poisoning Possible miscarriage of unborn baby	Sewage Dirty water Soil
Campylobacter	Poultry, milk, milk products	Severe, persistent abdominal pain Diarrhoea (often blood stained) Nausea Headache	Wild birds Animals Pests Water Sewage

Preventing FP – see the chart on pages 87–88 on how to avoid food poisoning.

Check your understanding
Tested

1 Identify four symptoms of food poisoning. *(4 marks)*
2 Name two food poisoning bacteria that could be found in meat. *(2 marks)*
3 Describe three ways to prevent food poisoning. *(6 marks)*

14.2 Food contamination

Key facts

Contamination is when unwanted substances (contaminants) make food unfit to eat, e.g.:

- micro-organisms
- hair, fingernails, nail varnish, jewellery
- skin infections or cuts, loose plasters
- nose or mouth mucus
- dirt and dust and soil
- dirty water
- chemicals, e.g. cleaning liquids, pesticide sprays
- pets or pests – insects (flies, maggots, etc.), rodents (rats, mice), bird droppings, fur, hairs, feathers, eggs
- small objects, e.g. packaging, glass, wood splinters.

Cross contamination means that micro-organisms transfer from one food to another by:

- **direct contact** – e.g. foods stored together
- **drips** – from raw food on to cooked foods
- **indirect contact** – hands, dishcloth, equipment, e.g. chopping board, knife, tongs.

> **Exam tip**
>
> When answering questions about reducing the risk of contamination or food poisoning, remember personal hygiene as well as food hygiene rules.

To avoid cross contamination and food poisoning

Rule or practice	How to follow it
Food storage	
Follow manufacturer's instructions	Read packaging for storage conditions, temperatures, 'use by' and 'best before' dates
Store perishable foods in a refrigerator	A refrigerator should have an internal temperature of 0–5°C
Store frozen perishable foods in a freezer	A freezer should have an internal temperature of at least −18°C
Store dry goods in sealed containers in a cool, ventilated cupboard	Keep away from any moisture and contamination from dust, dirt, pets and pests
Rotate the stock of foods	Use up old foods first before opening new ones
Store leftover foods in suitable containers in a cold place	• label with the date they were made • cool leftover food quickly – use within 24 hours, reheat thoroughly only once
Keep raw and cooked foods separate	In a refrigerator store raw foods on trays, plates or in covered containers underneath cooked foods (to prevent drip)
In a refrigerator, store salad ingredients and vegetables in a special box away from other foods	Wash the dirt off vegetables
Thaw frozen foods thoroughly before cooking them	Thaw frozen foods such as chicken on a tray in a refrigerator for several hours
Store food in a suitable cupboard	• keep food away from heat • ensure cupboard is free from pests • do not store food on the floor unless it is in sealed containers

(Continued)

Rule or practice	How to follow it
Food preparation	
Have clean hands	Wash your hands: • before cooking • after using the toilet • after handling raw meats, fish, dirty vegetables and eggs Keep fingernails short and clean; do not wear false nails, nail varnish, rings
Cover up cuts, sores or infections on hands	Wear a blue food grade plaster and a disposable plastic glove
Wear an apron or other clean covering	• wash the apron regularly • do not wear jewellery
Do not let hair fall into the food	Keep hair tied back or wear a hat
Do not contaminate food	• do not pick your nose, cough, sneeze or spit over food • do not smoke around food
Use clean equipment	• wash up regularly with hot soapy water, rinse, dry properly • use separate equipment for raw and cooked foods
Clear as you go	• throw away rubbish • clear work surfaces • wipe up spills • wash up between preparing raw food and cooked food • use clean dishcloths and drying cloths
Keep food covered and cool	• keep food in the refrigerator until needed • cover foods
Cooking food	
Cook perishable foods thoroughly	• make sure foods are cooked right through – at least 70°C for two minutes in the centre ('piping hot') • keep food hot to at least 63°C • use a temperature probe
Serving food	
Use clean plates, cutlery and serving dishes	• get rid of cracked plates and dishes • check forks are properly cleaned
Serve food hot	Serve food as soon as possible after cooking
Clearing up	
Wash up dishes and cutlery as soon as possible	• wash up with very hot water and detergent and rinse • check that awkward-shaped pieces of equipment, e.g. food processors, are thoroughly cleaned • regularly empty dishwasher filters
Use clean dishcloths and tea towels	• wash dishcloths and tea towels every day • dishcloths can be soaked in bleach for a few hours

Check your understanding — Tested

1 What is meant by the term 'cross contamination'? *(1 mark)*
2 Identify two ways contamination could occur. *(2 marks)*
3 Explain why you should defrost frozen food thoroughly before cooking it. *(4 marks)*

15 The role of food marketing and advertising

Key facts ─────────────────────────────────────

The food industry

- The food industry is a large industry employing many people.
- It is owned by a few big companies who make large profits from processing and selling food.

What is marketing?

- Marketing means identifying and supplying consumers' food **needs and wants**.
- **Market research** is:
  - finding out what consumers need and want
  - identifying **target groups** of people who might need or want particular food products
  - finding out what other manufacturers are making.
- Product development is:
  - making new food products and testing their popularity and acceptability
  - changing existing products
  - extending a range of products (e.g. introducing new flavours, reduced fat or salt versions).
- **Company positioning** means letting customers know where you stand on issues, e.g. environmental sustainability, animal welfare, fair trade, diet and health, local foods, additives, etc.
- **Advertising** is:
  - to promote products
  - **product launches**: special introductory price, buy one get one free (BOGOF), free samples, money-off vouchers, tasting sessions in shops
  - **image and brand building**: TV and internet adverts, exhibitions, street posters, leaflets, newspaper and magazine adverts, cinema adverts, adverts in shops, text messaging, mobile phone applications, telemarketing (call centres), radio promotions, using celebrities to promote a product.

↑ **Figure 15.1 Promoting a special offer**

↑ Figure 15.2 Free samples at the supermarket

Check your understanding ⎯⎯⎯⎯⎯⎯⎯⎯⎯⎯⎯⎯⎯ Tested ☐

1 State three ways a supermarket could advertise a new product in
store. *(3 marks)*

16 Purchasing (buying) foods

What makes people buy certain foods?

↑ **Figure 16.1**

Shopping trends

Shopping habits have changed over the years:

- Many small specialist food shops have closed in town centres.

- There has been some recent increased interest in specialist shops and markets (this has been encouraged by the media).

- Most food is purchased in supermarkets or out-of-town superstores.

- Food is purchased weekly rather than daily.

- Barcoding of food products.

- Online ordering and home delivery of food.

- Food from producer to consumer travels many miles from different countries (food miles).

- Many more convenience and ready-made meals or ingredients are sold and purchased.

- Increased use of packaging materials, especially plastics (sustainability and environmental implications).

↑ **Figure 16.2**

Exam tip

Think about why and how people purchase food as well as shopping trends.

Reasons for changes in shopping trends

● More women work outside home so there is less time for shopping or cooking.

● Car ownership means people can drive out of town for shopping.

● People's busy lives mean instantly available products are required.

● People travel abroad and try other food cultures and want to be able to buy similar foods at home.

● Technological changes.

● Influence of cookery programmes and food advertising.

● Fewer people feel confident and able to cook.

Exam tip

The reasons for people's eating habits are very varied; when answering questions on this, don't just think about price, think about areas such as:

● familiarity and dislikes

● being able to get to the shops

● are they able to cook (skill levels, elderly)?

● facilities at home

● working hours

● technological changes.

Check your understanding

Tested

1 Identify three factors that influence people when buying food.   *(3 marks)*

17 Food labelling

Key facts

- Labelling informs consumers about products.
- Labelling helps people with special dietary needs, e.g. a health condition, an allergy, a religious or cultural need.
- Labelling helps consumers keep foods safe to eat.

What information should be on food labels by law?

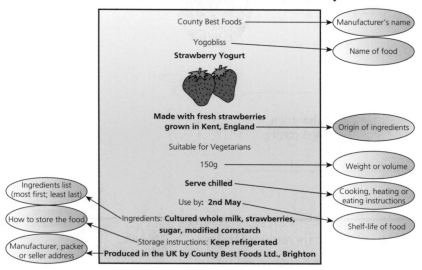

County Best Foods — Manufacturer's name

Yogobliss — Name of food
Strawberry Yogurt

Made with fresh strawberries grown in Kent, England — Origin of ingredients

Suitable for Vegetarians

150g — Weight or volume

Serve chilled — Cooking, heating or eating instructions

Use by: **2nd May**

Ingredients: **Cultured whole milk, strawberries, sugar, modified cornstarch** — Shelf-life of food

Storage instructions: **Keep refrigerated**
Produced in the UK by County Best Foods Ltd., Brighton

Ingredients list (most first; least last)

How to store the food

Manufacturer, packer or seller address

↑ **Figure 17.1**

Nutritional labelling

- Only compulsory if a claim is made, e.g. 'low fat', 'high fibre'.
- Nutrition information should be set out as a table or a list (not both together).
- A nutrition labelling table should look like this:

Exam tip

Remember, nutritional information is not required by law unless the food product makes a claim, e.g. 'low fat'.

Typical values	Per 100g	Per serving
Energy	kJ	kJ
	kcal	kcal
Protein	Total in g	Total in g
Fat	Total in g	Total in g
	of which saturates in g	of which saturates in g
Carbohydrate	Total in g	Total in g
	of which sugars in g	of which sugars in g
Fibre	Total in g	Total in g
Sodium	Total in g	Total in g
Salt equivalent	(grams of sodium × 2.5) Total in g	(grams of sodium × 2.5) Total in g

Nutritional labels may also show: sugars, starch, monounsaturates, polyunsaturates, cholesterol, vitamins, minerals, polyols.

Other information on labels

● Serving suggestions.

● Special offers.

● Symbols, e.g.:

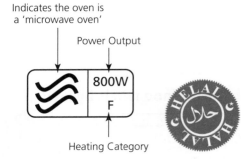

Indicates the oven is
a 'microwave oven'

Power Output

800W

F

Heating Category

↑ **Figure 17.2 Symbols used on food packaging**

> **Exam tip**
>
> A common mistake in exams is to describe a given symbol rather than
> state its meaning, e.g. for the Farm Assured Food Standards logo stating
> 'there is a tractor and flag showing it comes from a UK farm'.

Check your understanding
Tested

1 State three pieces of information on a food label that are required by law. *(3 marks)*

2 Describe how the nutritional information on a food product could be
   used by the consumer. *(4 marks)*

3 Identify three pieces of information someone wanting to lose weight could
   look for on a food product. *(3 marks)*

4 Name four nutrients listed on a nutritional label. *(4 marks)*

18 Food safety and the law

Key facts

- Laws protect consumers when buying food, e.g. The Food Hygiene (England) Regulations 2006 and The Food Safety Act and The Food Safety (General Food Hygiene) Regulations 1995.
- Laws ensure food is good quality and safe to eat.
- Enforced by:
  - central government
  - local government: Environmental Health Department and Trading Standards Department
  - Trading Standards Officers (deal with food labelling, composition, chemical contamination)
  - Environmental Health Officers (inspect food businesses, deal with hygiene, food poisoning, micro-organism contamination, unfit food); can close businesses down.
- If you have a **complaint** about a food: speak calmly and clearly to the shop/restaurant manager.
- If your complaint is not dealt with, then report this to an Environmental Health Officer or Trading Standards Officer.
- It is **against the law** (an offence) to:
  - sell unsafe food that could make people ill by infection from micro-organisms (this does not cover allergic reactions to food)
  - sell food unfit to eat, e.g. food that contains contaminants such as glass, chemicals
  - deliberately make food harmful
  - sell food that is not exactly as described or of a poor quality
  - mislead consumers about what the food actually contains or looks like, e.g. the food should match any photo of it on the packaging.

> **Exam tip**
> You do not need to know the laws in detail, just be aware of them.

Other consumer laws that cover food
- Trade Descriptions Act 1968
- Supply of Goods and Services Act 1982
- Sale and Supply of Goods Act 1994
- The Sale and Supply of Goods to Consumers Regulations 2002.

Check your understanding

1 Identify two ways a consumer is protected if they find that a food product is not of a satisfactory quality.

(2 marks)

Essay question

A growing number of people choose to be vegetarian. Explain why people choose to become vegetarian.   (8 marks)

Sample answer 1

There are 3 main reasons for people becoming vegetarians. Firstly, and most popularly of the 3, vegetarians have issues with the ethics of eating meat from animals who have been inhumaely killed or kept in bad conditions (for example, chickens in battery farms). Some also disagree with the animal feed, which is filled with hormones. The placing of these boundaries depends upon their beliefs. Incredibly strict vegetarians may refuse to eat yeast, wear wool or eat vegetables that require a plant to be killed in order to harvest the product. Secondly vegetarians may refuse to eat meat simply because they dislike the texture or taste. Another reason may be because of dietary specifications regarding hormones, cholesterol or preservatives. Finally, a minority of vegetarians have environmental issues with eating meat. They say that the farming of meat causes deforestation to create grazing land for the animals. In addition to these three categories, there are a number of other reasons for people becoming vegetarians.

Sample answer 2

There are a variety of reasons why somebody might choose a vegetarian diet. It could be due to heath, as some people believe a diet of cereals, vegetables, fruit, pulses and nuts along with milk products and eggs is healthier than one that contains meat and meat products. This may be linked to lower fat intake or people may think red meat is linked with higher cancer risk. People with religious beliefs may not be able to eat meat due to their traditions and culture. Some people may choose not to eat meat as they do not like the taste and texture of meat or fish. Allergy or intolerance are not usually a reason. Other people may think that it is wrong to kill animals for food and feel that the way animals are treated is cruel and wrong. Lastly people may believe that it is very expensive to produce meat products in relation to the production of cereal and crops. They may conscious of pollution and the effect meat production may have on the environment.

Commentary – reason for marks awarded   Revised ☐

When seeing an 'explain' question, look at the allocation of marks and then think of it as half the marks for identifying a point and the other half for a suitable explanation of that point. With this question the candidate is looking to provide a balanced answer in that they provide four reasons and then fully explain them. To get in the top level the answer needs to be structured and contain limited spelling, punctuation or grammar errors.

In **Sample Answer 1**, the candidate mentions:

1   Ethics and links to inhumane killing or bad conditions, with a good example.

2 Animal feed and hormones – this is a limited statement, further explanation is needed: why hormones are bad or why they would make someone become vegetarian. Knowledge is implied but not provided.

3 Irrelevant information about the degrees of vegetarianism and the types of vegetarians.

4 Dislike taste and texture.

5 Dietary specifications linked to hormones (repeat), cholesterol and pesticides. A good starting point but further information would be needed to fully explain this statement.

6 Environmental issues – creating grazing land causes deforestation; this statement is nearly there, a little more explanation would be needed to gain full marks.

7 Saying 'There are other reasons' is far too vague to gain any further accreditation.

The answer from candidate 1 was good and gave four reasons why people choose to become vegetarians but only explained two of these in enough detail, with some knowledge not fully applied. The answer was provided in a structured format. Some specialist terms were used. There were occasional errors in spelling, punctuation and grammar.

Total mark awarded: 5 out of 8

In **Sample Answer 2**, the candidate mentions:

1 Health reasons are linked to potentially consuming less fat.

2 This statement is then further explored as the candidate makes links to the media and stories relating to red meat and a potential increased risk of cancer, which may put people off eating meat. Although on the mark scheme this is also a separate point this can be considered an excellent demonstration of knowledge and linking to health reasons also.

3 Religion and saying that some traditions and cultures won't allow it is a good start but to get full credit the candidate should give an example of a religion that does not allow the eating of meat or a reason, such as that the pig is considered sacred.

4 Random statement about allergies and intolerances, which is correct but not relevant to the question being asked.

5 Wrong to kill animals and the way they are treated.

6 Economic reasons; this statement needs further clarification and explanation.

7 Environmental issues and pollution – this point also needs further explanation.

The candidate explained in detail why people may choose to follow a vegetarian diet. The answer given was detailed and accurate, with good explanations given. Six reasons for becoming vegetarian were given and three were fully explained, the other three needed a little further explanation, hence the candidate achieved the lower mark within this band and not full marks. The information was presented in a clear and organised way with specialist terms used where appropriate. There were few errors in spelling, punctuation and grammar.

Total mark awarded: 7 out of 8

Mark scheme for this question

This question is marked according to the quality of response. Candidates should be able to show their depth of understanding, using correct terminology.

If candidates respond by giving answers in a **list**, they remain in the **Level 2** response. Bullet point answers can only achieve up to Level 2.

The levels are:

- **Level 4 (7–8 marks)**: The candidate can explain in detail why people may choose to follow a vegetarian diet. The answers provided will be detailed and accurate. The information will be presented in a clear and organised way. A whole range of specialist terms are used with precision. There will be few errors in spelling, punctuation and grammar.

- **Level 3 (5–6 marks)**: The candidate can demonstrate some understanding by providing some explanation as to why people may choose to follow a vegetarian diet. Information will be offered to support the answer but in general terms with little detail. The information will be offered in a structured format. The candidate can use a range of specialist terms with facility. There may be occasional errors in spelling, punctuation and grammar.

- **Level 2 (3–4 marks)**: The candidate makes some limited explanations of why people may choose to follow a vegetarian diet. However, there may be some repetition of points/areas. Some information will be relevant, although it may lack specific detail. The candidate uses some specialist terms, although these may not always be used appropriately. There may be some errors in spelling, punctuation and grammar.

- **Level 1 (1–2 marks)**: The candidate makes vague comments about why people may choose to follow a vegetarian diet. Facts may not always relate to the content. Answers may be ambiguous or disorganised. There will be little or no use of specialist terms. Errors of grammar, punctuation and spellings may be intrusive. 0 means no response worthy of credit.

Specific information candidates may cover:

- **Religious belief(s)** – some religions set out grounds or rules regarding the consumption of meat and meat products; Islam, Hinduism, Buddhism, Judaism.

- **Objection to the slaughter of animals** – some people feel that the slaughter of animals is cruel or inappropriate.

- **More environmentally friendly or less economically wasteful** – belief that rearing animals is expensive, uses a lot of land, and/or contributes to global warming. Land could produce more food if used to grow cereal crops.

- **Dislike** – the taste or texture of animal flesh can put some people off.
- **Belief that vegetarianism is healthier** – higher in fibre and calcium and lower in fat and energy (energy density specifically). Some people can see the vegetarian diet as a more 'natural' diet and therefore choose to follow it for these reasons.
- **Pressure from other people** – it may be seen as a good thing to do or the rest of the family is vegetarian, therefore it is easier to cook one meal.
- **Media** – stories making links between higher incidences of cancers or other diseases and consumption of meat or fish.

Check your understanding answers

1.1–1.3 Nutrients: proteins, fat and carbohydrates

1   Milk, meat, fish, cheese, eggs, quinoa and soya beans.
2   For growth, repair, energy and maintenance of the body.
3   For insulation, protection, provides fat soluble vitamins (A, D, E, K), forms cell walls.
4   Fat that forms part of the food but cannot be seen.
5   Sucrose, fructose, glucose, galactose, lactose, maltose, invert sugar, hydrolysed starch.
6   Wholegrain cereal foods (whole wheat, brown rice, oats), wholegrain foods (pasta, bread, breakfast cereal, wheat and oat bran), seeds, beans, lentils, fruits, vegetables.

1.4–1.5 Vitamins

1   Cereals such as wheat and rice, wheatgerm, yeast, yeast extract, Marmite*, meat, eggs, fish roe, milk, cheese, yogurt, seeds, nuts, beans.
2   To help absorb iron, for the production of collagen/connective tissue, as antioxidant, protection of the body from chemicals and toxins (causing cell damage such as ageing).
3   Night blindness/keratomalacia.
4   Vitamin A (retinol), vitamin D (cholecalciferol), vitamin E (tocopherol), vitamin K.

1.6 Minerals and trace elements

1   Seafood, milk, dairy, some plants (depending on soil).
2   Normal growth, strengthens bones and teeth, enables bones to reach their peak bone mass, helps blood clot, normal function of nerves and muscles.

1.7–1.8 The importance of water and fibre in the diet

3   1.5 to 2 litres per day.
4   Chemical reactions in the body, found in all bodily fluids including joint fluids, controls body temperature, helps get rid of waste products, keeps the linings of the digestive system, mucous membrane and lungs moist, helps absorb nutrients, transports nutrients, maintains the correct concentration of electrolytes, helps protect the skin from drying out.
5   Helps in the removal of waste, ensures the intestines work properly, makes you feel full (satiated), reduces the cholesterol in the blood, stops constipation and diverticular disease, reduces the risk of some cancers.

2.1 Major diet-related health issues and conditions

1   When someone is receiving too much food or too much of one nutrient.

2   Obesity, cardiovascular disease (CVD), coronary heart disease (CHD), high blood pressure, diabetes, osteoporosis, cancer, anorexia, any deficiency disease (e.g. anaemia).
3   Eating fatty, salty and/or sugary foods, having a sedentary lifestyle, high stress levels, high or frequent intake of alcohol, smoking, being overweight or obese, high blood pressure, having a lot of fat around your waist, too much fat and cholesterol in your blood.

2.2 and 6 The relationship between diet and health

1   Base your meals on starchy foods, eat at least five portions of fruit and vegetables per day, eat more (oily) fish, cut down on fat (especially saturated), cut down on sugar, eat less salt, get active, try to maintain a healthy weight, drink at least 2 litres of water per day, do not skip breakfast.
2   Five.
3   Check food labels for sugar content, buy reduced sugar products, do not add sugar to foods or beverages, use an artificial sweetener instead, use naturally sweet foods to add flavour, reduce the amount of sugar in recipes.
4   A diet that contains a wide variety of food containing different nutrients; the right amount of nutrients for your needs; a variety of natural food textures, flavours and/or colours.
5   Different likes and dislikes, lack of time to cook/prepare/shop for food, not eating at home, limited money, limited cooking skills, lack of space to prepare/cook/store food.

2.3 Recommended daily amounts of nutrients

1   Dietary reference value(s).

3 Energy and food

1   ● Age – metabolic rate and physical activity reduce as we age.
    ● Gender – males usually require more energy.
    ● Physical activity/job/lifestyle – being active in your spare time, e.g. a marathon runner, or having a physically demanding job, e.g. a builder, requires more energy.
    ● Pregnancy – pregnant women have a higher energy requirement.
    ● Health – if someone has a broken leg and is therefore inactive, they will require less energy.
    ● Body composition – a higher fat-free mass (muscle) requires more energy as muscle burns more energy.
2   Calories, kilocalories, joules, kilojoules.
3   They will put on weight or fat.
4   They will have an increased risk of: diabetes, CHD, CVD, high blood pressure, increased cholesterol.

4.1 Meat and poultry

1   Protein, fat, vitamin A, vitamin D, group B vitamins and iron.
2   Contains a high level of vitamin A, which is harmful or toxic to the baby.
3   Insert a temperature probe into the middle to see if the centre is above the danger zone (5–63°C). The core temperature

should be 70°C for 2 minutes or 75°C for 30 seconds. Place a knife into the centre and the juice should remain clear.

4.2 Fish and seafood

4 Protein, fat, vitamin A, vitamin D, group B vitamins, calcium, omega-3, fluoride and iodine.

5 Contains omega 3, which is good for heart health, omega 3 also has positive effects on diseases such as dementia (brain health) and cardiovascular health, it is one of the healthy eating guidelines, omega 3 is important for the development of the central nervous system.

4.3 Eggs

1 Circle protein, fat, vitamin A, calcium and iron.

4.4 Milk

2 Vitamin A, vitamin D.

3 Soya, coconut, rice, goat's or oat milks.

4.5 Dairy products

4 A food that perishes quickly and usually contains a high amount of water.

5 The yogurt is within its use by date, the lid has not 'blown' or split, and when opened the yogurt does not smell 'off' or look mouldy.

4.6 Fruits and vegetables

1 Carrots, red peppers, oranges, palm fruit, dark green leafy vegetables, tomatoes and apricots.

2 Encourage them to help with the cooking or preparing; grow your own; make attractive designs on the plate; eat with them; provide a variety to try; cut into small pieces; have raw and cooked versions; introduce fruits and vegetables at a young age; introduce new flavours more than once; make smoothies; have as puddings; read books about fruits and vegetables.

3 It is in date, not bruised, has no mould, has not shrunk in size, wilted or been damaged, nutritional value, store in cool and dark place (potatoes go green if left in light meaning they are poisonous to eat), always wash before using and eating.

4.7 Cereals and cereal products

1 Protein, carbohydrate, group B vitamins, fat, iron, vitamin E and fibre.

2 Barley, buckwheat, corn (maize), millet, oats, quinoa, rice, rye, spelt and wheat.

3 Wheat flour contains gluten. They cannot digest or are allergic to gluten.

4.8 Sugars and sweeteners

1 For flavour, taste, texture, colour, preservation, to trap air, to make a mixture, to make it light.

2 Use half sucrose and half sweetener, or add a naturally sweet fruit.

5.1 Convenience foods

1 ● Advantages – quick or little preparation, time saving, single portion or portion-controlled, less waste, limited or no skills needed, require little space to cook or store, could be cheaper.

● Disadvantages – can be more expensive, lots of packaging (has an effect on the environment and non-renewable resources), nutritional concerns (convenience foods can have a greater amount of fat, sugar, salt and energy, which causes concern for healthcare professionals), a decline in the number of people being able to cook (people are not using their skills to cook, therefore there is a greater reliance on convenience foods).

5.2 Genetically modified foods

2 Longer shelf life, greater resistance to disease/pests, faster growing, greater number of products per plant, better resistance to weed-killing chemicals, better nutritional quality.

5.3 Organic foods

3 People think it tastes better, concerns about the pesticides used (and the effect on our health and the environment), concerns over intense farming methods, people think they contain more nutrients, greater availability, greater publicity.

4 A food which is produced using organic farming methods, such as without the use of chemicals or pesticides.

5.4 Functional foods

1 Greater publicity, greater availability, more health conscious, cheaper prices.

2 ● Whole oat products, soya beans, plant stanols – lowers blood cholesterol, reduces the risk of developing heart disease.

● Oily fish, omega 3 – reduces the risk of heart disease, reduces the risk of Alzheimer's.

● Cranberry juice – reduces the risk of urinary tract infections.

● Green tea – reduces the risk of developing some cancers.

● Tomatoes and tomato products – reduces the risk of developing some cancers (especially prostate).

● Dark green leafy vegetables – reduces the risk of developing eye illness.

● Probiotics – beneficial effects on the intestines and immune system.

● Beetroot juice – increased endurance capacity.

3 A food you would eat as part of a normal diet that contains naturally occurring substances that can decrease your risk of developing certain diseases and enhance your general health. Additional benefits over nutrition only.

7.1 Babies and children

1 Breast milk or formula milk.

2 Peanuts, wheat, egg, soya, shellfish, nuts, fish.

3 For growth and repair.

7.2 Teenagers

1 Iron, vitamin C and protein.

2 Vitamin C.

3 Meat, fish, beans, lentils, tofu, beans, Quorn®, eggs, soya.

4 Cheese, milk, bread, yogurt, seeds, nuts, lentils, enriched fruit juices.

7.3 Adults and senior citizens

1 Lack of exercise limits the stimulation of the bones to take up calcium, bones naturally lose minerals and become weaker as they age, lack of exposure to the sun, lack of dietary intake or decreased appetite, reduced vitamin D absorption.

2 False.

3 ● Lack of appetite – so choose not to eat or only eat small amounts.

   ● Lack of ability (dexterity) – can only stand for a limited time so cooks only simple meals or meals requiring little preparation.

   ● Lack of facilities – they may only have a microwave so are limited in what they can cook.

   ● Likes and dislikes not taken into consideration – living in a care home or having others cooking for them.

   ● Lack of skill – if living on their own and/or their partner who always cooked for them has died.

   ● Oral/mouth problems – eating is hard so they choose not to eat or eat only soft foods.

   ● Lack of money to buy food – limited variety or only cheap foods such as pasta and no fruit or vegetables.

   ● Lack of ability to get to the shops to purchase food – only able to buy what is in local stores.

   ● Poor absorption of nutrients – ageing decreases absorption rates.

   ● Changes in sense(s) – may come to dislike the smell or taste of certain foods.

4 Calcium, vitamin D.

7.4 Pregnant women

1 Reduces the risk of the baby developing spina bifida or neural tube defects.

2 Pâté, soft cheeses, raw or lightly cooked meat, liver or liver products, raw or partly cooked eggs, some fish (shark, swordfish, tuna, marlin), alcohol and caffeine.

3 ● Pâté – can contain Listeria, which may cause illness in the mother and harm the baby.

   ● Soft cheeses – these have a higher risk of food poisoning and therefore may harm the mother and baby.

   ● Raw or lightly cooked meat – undercooked meat contains bacteria, which could cause food poisoning.

   ● Liver or liver products – liver contains high levels of vitamin A, which may harm the baby.

   ● Raw or partly cooked eggs – may contain Salmonella, which could harm the mother and baby.

   ● Some fish – can contain high levels of mercury, which would harm the development of the baby's brain and nervous system.

   ● Alcohol and caffeine – could cause the baby to be underweight when born.

7.5 People trying to lose weight

1 Increased risk of heart disease, diabetes, high blood pressure, osteoarthritis, joint problems, feeling low or depressed or not wanting to socialise, problems having surgery because there is fat under the skin, breathing difficulties, skin rashes or infections, personal hygiene problems due to fat folds increasing the difficulty of washing, mobility problems or limited exercise opportunities.

2 Eating too much (more energy than they use), not doing enough exercise, diets or commercial weight loss products that have caused them to gain weight, diet cycling, eating high fat or high energy foods, snacking, increased portion size, having a less active job, medical, e.g. steroids, genetic predisposition.

3 Eat less energy-/fat-/sugar-dense foods, eat low energy foods, change cooking methods (grilling rather than frying), reduce portion size, eat low fat products, be more active.

7.6 Vegetarians

1 Do not like the idea of eating the flesh of a dead animal, disagree with the raising of animals for slaughter, feel that rearing animals is a waste of resources, which if used for crops could feed more people, feel it is a healthier diet, religious or cultural reasons, pressure from others or another member of the family is a vegetarian, dislike the taste or texture of meat or fish, think it is cheaper.

2 Eggs, tofu, beans, lentils, Quorn®, tempeh, nuts, seeds, peas.

3 Fortified foods such as yeast extract, soya milk, sunflower margarine and breakfast cereals.

7.7 Coeliacs

1 Ground almonds, buckwheat flour, ground chestnuts, corn (maize), gram flour, ground mustard, ground peas, ground lentils, potato flour, rice flour, urd/urid.

2 Weight loss, lack of energy, tiredness, diarrhoea, anaemia – poor absorption of iron and vitamin C, poor growth, and general malnutrition.

7.8 Diabetics

3 True.

4 ● Only a small amount of sugary foods to be eaten, preferably as part of a meal rather than as a single food. No need to buy specialist 'diabetic foods' as they are often unbalanced in terms of dietary guidelines, e.g. contain high levels of fat. Avoid dried fruits and fruit in sugar or syrup.

   ● Reduce the sugar content of sugary foods, for example in recipes replace some sugar with naturally sweet foods.

   ● Complex carbohydrates, such as wholemeal pasta, brown rice, wholemeal bread, sweet potatoes, should be the main base of meals. They provide energy that is slowly released, which helps to control blood sugar levels and satiety (reduced need to snack). Follow the GI diet or eat low GI foods.

   ● Control/reduce fat intake as diabetics have a greater risk of developing heart disease. Take measures such as choosing lean cuts of meat or trimming fat off meat, and grilling rather than frying or roasting in fat. Choose low fat dairy products.

   ● Control or reduce salt/sodium intake, which helps control or reduce blood pressure and reduce the risk of developing heart disease. Choose low salt versions of foods and use other ingredients such as herbs for flavourings.

- Increase fruit and vegetable intake, which will help control blood sugar levels, and also provide a range of vitamins and minerals including antioxidants, which reduce the risk of many diseases including heart disease.

5 Ensure they know how much sugar is in the food and therefore the effect this will have on their blood sugar. Sugar is often hidden and labelled as other things such as glucose or fructose and they need to be able to recognise other names.

7.9 Food allergies and intolerances

1 It is the body having an allergic reaction to a food or ingredient.

2 Eggs, peanuts, other nuts, seeds, strawberries, kiwi fruit, oranges, seafood, wheat bread, flour, gluten, soya, cow's milk, lactose, tartrazine, monosodium glutamate (MSG), spices, tomatoes.

3 A non-allergic reaction to a food. Intolerances do not involve an immune system reaction and are less likely to have severe symptoms.

7.10 Coronary heart disease

1 Build-up of fat in the arteries, eating a lot of saturated fat, having a high amount of low density lipoproteins (bad) cholesterol, high cholesterol, smoking, high blood pressure, being overweight or obese, a sedentary lifestyle, not eating enough fruit and/or vegetables, having a low fibre intake.

2
- Stop smoking cigarettes or at least reduce the number smoked.
- Take more exercise (especially aerobic) to increase oxygen intake; this may also help with weight loss and reduction of blood pressure.
- Eat more fruit and vegetables, at least five a day and eat a variety to ensure an adequate intake of antioxidants.
- Eat less saturated fat and increase unsaturated fat intake, choose leaner cuts of meat, reduce intake of foods such as cheese, butter and solid vegetable fats.
- Lose weight, through reducing energy intake and/or becoming more active by increasing either our exercise or daily physical activity.
- Eat more fibre by eating more fruit and vegetables and wholemeal foods.
- Eat a balanced diet.
- Reduce salt intake, e.g. use different herbs and spices to flavour foods.

8.1 Social and economic diversity

1
- Use cheaper cuts of meat. Tenderise the meat by stewing or slow cooking.
- Add alternative protein sources such as beans and lentils to make meals go further (bulk out meals).
- Make food from scratch rather than buying pre-prepared foods or ingredients.
- Use produce in season.
- Take advantage of special offers, such as buy one get one free.
- Make meals in bulk and freeze them for when you are in a hurry.
- Purchase some ingredients in bulk.

- Use supermarket own brands or cheaper brands.
- Collect coupons and money-off offers.
- Use tinned or frozen fruits and vegetables.
- Use the freezer to take advantage of offers and cooking in bulk.

2 Ensure you have a minimum of four of the following elements:
- At least two portions of fruits and/or vegetables.
- A carbohydrate source.
- A protein source – maybe a cheaper cut of meat or pulses to bulk out foods.
- Low fat foods or food cooked in a way to reduce fat intake, e.g. not deep fried.
- Think about cooking methods – cheaper ways of cooking, such as one pot meals.
- Food costs, such as a cheaper cut of meat or frozen vegetables.
- Not relying on convenience foods.
- Taking advantage of special offers in store.
- Things that smaller children would be happy to eat, e.g. not too spicy or specialist foods.
- Two courses, including a main course.
- Must be reference to the cost or how the cost has been reduced.
- Balanced – not high in fat or salt.
- Cooked from scratch (where appropriate – wouldn't expect people to cook pasta from scratch or do things that require expensive equipment).

8.2 Cultural and religious diversity

1 Changes:
- Where people shop – people shop in large/all-in-one shops rather than in smaller specialist shops.
- Frequency of shopping – people tend to do a weekly shop rather than more frequent shops.
- How people shop – online ordering and 'click and collect' have become more popular.
- Greater availability of foreign or unusual foods.
- Many products are available all year.
- Products travel large distances, greater food miles.
- More convenience products are available.
- People are more conscious or aware of the environment and animal welfare so things such as organic foods and welfare rights have come about.
- People look for healthier options.
- More options for home delivery, e.g. meals on wheels for the elderly.
- Cost of foods (ranges suitable for all budgets).
- Eating on the move, fast foods, convenience foods.
- Awareness of health, intolerances, allergies.
  Reasons (mix and match to the above changes, some are appropriate for more than one change):
- More large supermarkets have opened, therefore driving out the smaller and specialist shops. Less able to shop locally.

- More people own cars so they can travel to out-of-town supermarkets.
- Larger stores can offer cheaper prices as they buy in bulk, which is attractive for all consumers.
- People have less time, so demand is increased for 'all-under-one-roof shopping'.
- People are working longer hours and women are working as well as men, therefore there is less time to shop.
- People lead busy lives, therefore there is an increasing need to have things instantly and fast.
- Technology has changed so we are able to buy foods without visiting a shop.
- Technology has also changed meaning foods have a longer shelf life, best before, use by date. This means we can buy foods less frequently to be consumed later in the week.
- Changing technology is also a reason why we are able to have strawberries all year – packaging, air freight.
- There are greater opportunities for travel and experiencing foods from other countries and cultures, which creates demand.
- We now live in a multicultural society, therefore the supermarkets are providing foods to suit the ethnic backgrounds of the local residents.
- There has been a gradual decline in the number of people feeling confident or having the knowledge to cook from scratch.
- More cookery programmes and books mean more people want to try new foods and recipes.
- More programmes about ethical and cultural issues.
- Greater awareness of government advice.
- Ageing population meaning greater need for such services.
- Awareness of health, intolerances, allergies has created a greater range of products.
- Ranges of foods are suitable for all budgets, e.g. low cost supermarket own brands to luxury brands.

2 Buddhism, Hinduism and Sikhism.

9.1 The transfer of heat to foods

1 To destroy harmful bacteria or poisons, to develop flavours, to make food easier to chew, swallow and digest, make food more appetising, variety of food, heat food when it is cold, to make the product, e.g. a cake.

2 Conduction, convection and radiation.

3
- Conduction → the passing of heat through solid materials such as metal or food.
- Convection → the passing of heat through a gas or a liquid.
- Radiation → the passing of heat through a space without the use of a solid, liquid or gas.

9.2 Grilling, frying, roasting, baking and barbecuing

1 By radiation.

2 There is no added fat, when grilling the fat melts and drains off the food.

3 Protection, to add flavour, add texture, hold the fish together, add colour.

4 Only a little oil is added, it is a quicker cooking method so fewer vitamins and minerals are destroyed.

5
- Wash hands after going to the toilet and between handling different types of food – avoid cross contamination.
- Store foods out of the danger zone – bacteria grows faster in the danger zone, increasing the risk of food poisoning.
- Best before date should be adhered to – after this date the food is likely to contain more bacteria and increases the risk of food poisoning.
- Store raw and cooked foods separately – reduces the chance of cross contamination.
- Use separate utensils for raw and cooked food.
- Store foods according to instructions – keep out of the danger zone, decreases the risk of food going off before the best before date.
- Make sure food is cooked right the way through – meat should not contain blood, if food is not cooked long enough over a hot enough heat the bacteria will not be destroyed.
- Food should be cooked over a high heat so that the bacteria are destroyed and the core temperature reaches at least 72°C. Check with a thermometer.
- Coals need regulating so the outside is not burnt before the inside is cooked.
- Keep food covered – reduces the chance of cross contamination or contact with contaminated air particles or pests.
- Clean utensils and barbecue and clean surfaces to minimise cross contamination.
- Pre-cook food indoors before putting on the barbecue to ensure that it is cooked thoroughly, especially for thick cuts of meat.

9.3 Boiling, poaching, simmering, steaming, stewing, braising and microwaving

1 Steaming, microwaving, stir-frying.

2 Stewing, braising, slow cooking.

3 Economical, quick, can be healthier, cooks a large variety of foods, space saving, saves washing up, pre-set accurate timings available.

10.1 Basic ingredients

1 As a spread, shortening, frosting, flavouring, for moisture and to trap air.

2 To trap air, to bind ingredients, to coat a product (protection), to thicken, emulsify, glaze, enrich, and to garnish.

3 Sauces, such as an egg custard sauce.

4 To add sweetness, for texture, to trap air, to add colour.

5 To add air to the mixture, help the mixture rise.

6 Coriander, kaffir lime leaves, cardamom (seeds), cayenne pepper, cumin, turmeric.

10.2 The use of raising agents in cooking

1 Sieving flour, creaming fat, whisking eggs, folding or rolling a mixture, rubbing fat into flour.

2 ● Bread contains yeast, a raising agent.

● Yeast, given the correct conditions (food, warmth, time and moisture), converts food into carbon dioxide.

● Carbon dioxide is a gas, meaning it expands and pushes the dough mixture upwards.

● Carbon dioxide creates a larger volume and less dense texture.

● This process is known as fermentation or proving.

3 Baking powder, yeast.

11.1 Cooking breads, pastries, cakes, biscuits and scones

1 ● When the pastry dough is put into a hot oven, the fat melts.

● The fat is absorbed by the starch in the flour.

● Folding introduces air to the mixture. The air that is trapped between the layers of dough expands and pushes up the dough.

● Water is added to the mixture to bind.

● The water in the dough turns to steam, which also pushes up the dough.

● The gluten and starch set and the pastry becomes crisp and flaky.

2 Golden colour, light texture, soft.

3 ● Colour – the mixture goes from pale to darker in colour.

● Texture – the mixture forms an airy structure and on the outside a golden crust is formed.

● Taste – the baking brings out a different flavour.

● Rises – the air in the mixture causes it to rise. Air holes are created, forming an aerated structure.

● If used, chocolate melts and fruit softens giving a different texture and flavour.

4 To absorb the fat, give texture and give a 'melt in the mouth' flavour.

5 True.

11.2 Cooking sauces and batters

1 To add liquid, flavour, colour, to bind ingredients, to add nutrients, to make meals more varied and interesting.

2 ● Starch gelatinises.

● When starch is heated in a liquid, the liquid passes through the walls of the starch granules.

● The granules become swollen and burst.

● This is gelatinisation.

● When starch is heated it absorbs the liquid and thus thickens the sauce.

3 Egg, flour, milk/water.

4 ● The liquid – turns to steam and pushes the mixture up so it rises.

● The protein – sets the mixture.

● The starch – the wheat protein sets the mixture. The starch also absorbs some of the liquid and oil, which again helps the mixture to set.

11.3 Cooking meat, poultry and fish

1 ● Texture change – the meat becomes firmer, shrinks and can become tender.

● Flavour changes – the fat melts, creating flavour and moisture. The fat can also be cooked to make it crispy. Meat extractives are also created (meat juice) giving a greater flavour. If it is cooked in a stew the meat can take on the flavour of the other ingredients in the stew.

● Colour – poultry becomes white and red meats become brown.

● Size change – the meat shrinks due to fat loss.

2 The juices should run clear (no blood) when a knife is placed into the chicken. The meat will also be a white colour rather than the pink it was before cooking. Use a thermometer – the centre temperature should be 72°C for 2 minutes or 75°C for 30 seconds.

11.4 Cooking vegetables and fruit

1 Boiling, simmering, steaming, stewing, stir-frying, frying, roasting, baking, microwaving.

2 ● Texture changes – the carrot softens.

● Flavour – the flavour intensifies and becomes sweeter.

● Nutritional value – water destroys the vitamin C, beta carotene is more readily available to the body.

3 Do not prepare until needed, cut into larger chunks, peel thinly, do not soak, leave skins on and tear up leafy vegetables.

11.5 The effects of acids and alkalis on food

1 Lemon juice or vinegar.

2 As a preservative, as an antioxidant, to enable cooking processes to work, to alter the texture of some food, to prevent some fruits going brown.

3 Bicarbonate of soda.

12 The function of additives in food products

1 As a preservative, for colouring, for flavouring or sweetness, as an emulsifier or stabiliser or as a thickener.

2 Calcium, iron, thiamine (B_1), riboflavin (B_2) and niacin (B_3).

13.1 Food spoilage

1 Milk, meat, poultry, fish, seafood, cream, eggs, soft fruits (e.g. strawberries and raspberries), sauces, soups and gravies.

2 ● Display until date → the food must be sold by this date (but is still safe to eat after this date).

● Use by date → the date by which the food should be eaten to ensure it is safe.

● Best before date → the food will be at its best condition before this date (relates to flavour/texture).

13.2 Food preservation at home

1 Kills micro-organisms by removing water, prevents some chemical reactions taking place, stops micro-organism growth as they need water/moisture to grow.

2 Cabbage, gherkins, onions, fruits, herrings and hard boiled eggs.

13.3 Commercial food preservation

1 Canning, fluid bed freezing, air-blast freezing, cryogenic freezing, salting, vacuum packaging.

2 Micro-organisms cannot grow in high concentrations of salt; the salt dehydrates the micro-organisms by removing water. Micro-organisms need water for growth.

14.1 Causes and effects of food poisoning

1 Nausea, vomiting, abdominal cramps, diarrhoea, high or low body temperature, headache, general aching of the body, weakness and lack of energy, trouble breathing or swallowing.

2 Salmonella, Staphylococcus aureus, Bacillus cereus, Escherichia coli (E. coli), Clostridium perfringens, Listeria monocytogenes, Campylobacter.

3 ● Store food correctly – in the correct place, at the correct temperature, for the correct amount of time, in suitable containers or packaging, defrost thoroughly.

● Handle food hygienically – wear clean clothing, wash your hands, use clean equipment, do not allow raw food to come into contact with cooked food, do not touch your body and then handle food, do not let animals or pests contaminate it.

● Cook food properly and thoroughly – to the right temperature, for the right amount of time, keep it hot before serving, cool leftover food quickly, use leftovers within 24 hours and reheat only once.

● Clean properly – clean regularly as you prepare and cook, clear away rubbish regularly, use clean dishcloths and drying up cloths, clean equipment in hot soapy water and dry thoroughly, keep food cupboards and refrigerators clean, keep pests out of the kitchen.

14.2 Food contamination

1 Allowing micro-organisms to transfer from one food to another (usually raw to cooked). This can be through direct contact, drips, indirect contact.

2 ● Through micro-organisms.

● Hair, fingernails, skin, nail varnish, jewellery falling into food.

● Skin cuts and infections transferring micro-organisms.

● Jewellery can contain trapped dirt.

● Coughing or sneezing over the food – mucus from the lining of the nose, mouth and saliva.

● Dirt and dust (airborne).

● Chemicals, such as cleaning fluids.

● Pests and pets transferring dirt and bacteria.

● Small objects, such as glass and plastic, falling into food.

● Direct contact between two foods, e.g. raw meat and cooked meat touching.

● Drips from raw food dripping from a top shelf on to food below.

● Indirect contact – where micro-organisms have been transferred by hands, dishcloths or equipment used for more than one food.

3 Bacteria will remain alive in the cold centre part of the unthawed food while it is cooking. They will start to reproduce because the food may not get hot enough in the centre to kill them. They could then cause food poisoning.

15 The role of food marketing and advertising

1 In-store announcements, taste session or samples, offers such as buy one get one free, end-of-aisle displays, product placement, wobblers, celebrity endorsement, flyers, money off coupons, colourful packaging, posters, recommendations from staff, staff handing out information, staff dressing up.

16 Purchasing (buying) foods

1 Price/offers, familiarity of a product, reputation of a product, supermarket or brand, recommendation, availability of a product, use by or sell by dates, lifestyle, e.g. time factors, special diets, advertising, celebrity endorsement, occasions or traditions, personal likes/dislikes, religion, culture or ethnicity, organic, fair trade, personal skill levels, facilities available (storage and preparation), environmental issues, carbon foot print, sustainability, animal welfare or safety, portion size, packaging, season, appearance of the food.

17 Food labelling

1 ● Name of the product.

● List of ingredients (in descending order of weight).

● Additives.

● Net quantity, weight of the product, volume.

● Instructions about storage.

● Instructions about cooking, use, how to make the product.

● Contact address, manufacturer address, how to contact the manufacturer.

● Name of manufacturer.

● How long the food will last, date mark, shelf life, use by date, best before date, date code, display until.

● Place of origin, where the product was made.

● Nutritional information relating to any claim that has been made.

● Description of the food product.

● Allergy information.

2 ● To compare products – whether one contains more or less of a particular nutrient or ingredient.

● To help choose a product – look for higher fibre, lower fat, salt, sugar product.

- To help make informed judgements and choices about whether any claims are justified.
- As a guide – for example, to provide a guide to portion sizes as part of a balanced diet or for weight loss.
- For allergy information – see if there are any ingredients they are allergic to.
- To provide help on a calorie controlled diet.
- To help choose the correct nutrients.
- Monitor nutrient intake.

3 Energy (kcal or kJ) per portion, sugar content, fat content, if they are on a commercial diet the commercial companies' information.

4 Energy (kcal or kJ), protein, carbohydrates (and of which are sugars), fat (and of which are saturates), fibre, sodium, sugars, polyols, starch, monounsaturates, polyunsaturates, cholesterol, vitamin and minerals.

18 Food safety and the law

1
- Can take the product back to the store where it was bought – store has to look into the problem.
- Proof of purchase would be required – shows when they bought the item.
- Best before date should not be exceeded – if the product has deteriorated before this time the customer is allowed to take the product back.
- A refund, replacement, credit note or alternative item should be offered – dependent on consumer preference.
- Protected by laws such as the 'Trade Descriptions Act'.
- Citizens Advice Bureau (CAB) can advise.
- Supermarkets will want to seem helpful for the sake of their reputation.
- Environmental Health Officers can advise or help and/or investigate.

Index